ELVIS COSTELLO:
A Man Out Of Time

ELVIS COSTELLO:
A Man Out Of Time

A Critical Companion to His Lyrics and Music

David Gouldstone

SIDGWICK & JACKSON
LONDON

First published in Great Britain in 1989 by Sidgwick & Jackson Limited

Copyright © 1989 by David Gouldstone

ISBN 0–283–99707–9

Typeset by Input Typesetting Ltd, London
Printed by Mackays of Chatham PLC, Letchworth
for Sidgwick & Jackson Limited
1 Tavistock Chambers, Bloomsbury Way
London WC1A 2SG

To my mother and father

Contents

Acknowledgements

I should like to thank Tim Birt, who discussed the early stages of this book with me, Bob Jackson, who kindly allowed me to write some of it in his house, and most of all Sue, who did the typing and contributed more than she probably realises.

Preface

Elvis Costello is widely regarded as one of rock's finest song-writers. It is well over a decade now since his first records appeared, part of the new wave of British rock music in the late 1970s. Most of the other singers and groups who surfed to success then, including many talented musicians, have since been washed away by the tide and forgotten, but a few coast on. Of these some balance precariously as they approach the late eighties, but Costello's stance is assured. After quickly making a name for himself with a remarkable debut album, he went on to consolidate his position by releasing a series of diverse and dauntingly good records. On these records his reputation rests. His status is, surely, impregnable; anyone who listens to the songs he's written since 1977 must agree that he is a talent to be taken seriously.

The purpose of this book is to act as a kind of guide to these songs. When we look around, say, a city, we often do so guide book in hand; its function is to point out the places of interest, to tell us something about them and to put them in a context. In short, guide books help us to enjoy our visit. This is how I intend this book to be used. I hope that by reading what I've written about particular songs or albums the listener will hear details that he or she had perhaps not noticed before, or come to understand better the connection between the details. In this way listeners will, I hope, gain a deeper and fuller appreciation of Costello's music, and so get more pleasure from it. His imaginative landscape is in some ways very complex, and this book tries to provide a map to lead the listener through the sometimes labyrinthine twists and turns of his songs.

This book is a companion to Costello's lyrics and music. It is not a biography; I have made no attempt to psychoanalyse him by dirty-raincoating through his songs looking for 'clues' to his supposed disorders and traumas. He is entitled to his privacy, and besides, I am deeply suspicious of critical methods that are more concerned with the artist than the artefact. What I have tried to do is to listen carefully to his songs and then write about them *as songs*, not as fragments of putative autobiography. Occasionally I have referred to events in his life, but only when it's necessary for the complete understanding of a song and when the events are already public knowledge. Otherwise I am not much interested in Costello as a man; the reader is of course free to try to draw his or her own conclusions about him from his songs if he or she wishes. (I should point out that this book was not written with his co-operation, and so my comments are in no sense 'official'.)

The subtitle of this book puts 'Lyrics and Music' in that order deliberately. Its emphasis is on the lyrics rather than the music. This is firstly because music is impossible to write about at length without being either vague or technical. Vagueness is something all writers should avoid, and I wouldn't want to write a technical book even if I were capable of doing so. (The few musical terms that I use are either explained as I go along or are self-explanatory in their context.) But the second and most important reason is that it is chiefly on his lyrics that Costello's reputation is founded. Naturally it's his music that initially attracts people to his songs, but by and large it's the words that make them stay. It's quite common to hear him described as rock's best lyricist after Bob Dylan, and while I'm not entirely happy about pigeon-holing artists and putting them in pecking orders this is a pretty fair assessment of his status. Plenty of other rock songwriters have written good lyrics too, but not so consistently over such a long period as Costello and Dylan.

It's a shame that it's necessary to separate lyrics and music for the sake of the discussion, though almost inevitable. In a way it's wrong to break down a song, or any other artefact, into its constituent parts. It was conceived as a unity, and if it works at all must work as a unity. But look at it this way: separating the lyrics and music is similar to devoting separate sections in a bicycle repair manual to, say, the frame and the wheels. It's just a matter of convenience. No one supposes that a frame or a wheel is of any use by itself, and it's only when the parts of the bike or song are put together that they can function: they move.

I've sometimes discussed the lyrics with little or no reference to the music which goes with them, for reasons that I've tried to explain. There is a danger in this critical approach, though, which I've constantly had in mind (but maybe not always managed to avoid) and of which the reader should beware. The danger is treating the lyrics as if they were poetry. They are not poetry, and should not be read as such. This is not intended to be a slur on their quality – after all, there's good and bad poetry, so calling something 'poetry' says nothing about its value – but is a simple statement of how they are meant to be heard. 'Heard' is the right word to use. Despite it being the fashion to sprawl groups' illiteracies all over their album sleeves, Costello's lyrics were not printed with the record until *Imperial Bedroom*, five years into his recording career. Although they often have the density of expression and controlled ambiguity of good poetry they can't be appreciated properly without listening to them as part of a song.

If at times it appears that I've made a Montaigne out of a *Mill Hill Chronicle* by reading too much into a lyric, I ask the reader to listen to the setting of the lyric before dismissing what I've said. Often the full significance of the words is apparent only when heard. For example, in my discussion of 'No Dancing', from *My Aim Is True*, I come close to claiming that the narrator of the song's phrase 'somebody has to cry' means something not very far removed from King Lear's 'when we are born, we cry that we are come to this great stage of fools.' No one in their right mind would claim that Costello comes within a million miles of matching the significance of Shakespeare's line *on paper*, but listen to the way he sings his line and it's a completely different matter. The music of songs endows the lyrics with nuance and significance they wouldn't otherwise possess.

In discussing the songs I have used names for their various sections which are usually self-explanatory, but to prevent any possible confusion I shall define my terms here. The 'verse' of a song usually comes first (unless there's a preliminary introduction). Verses almost never repeat their lyric; in other words every time the tune of the verse is heard it's accompanied by different words. (Repeating verses is a technique very frequently used by lesser songwriters to spin their songs out, but '(I Don't Want To Go To) Chelsea' is almost the only example of Costello doing this.) The 'chorus', however, usually keeps the same lyric throughout the song; in other words every time the tune of the chorus is heard it's accompanied by the same words.

I use 'verse' and 'chorus' in accordance with common usage, which might not quite be the case with another term I often use, 'middle'. A song's middle is often crucial, so it's important that I make clear exactly what I mean by this term. The main identifying features of a middle are that it comes immediately after the chorus, and that *its tune and lyric are heard once only*. Just to confuse the issue there are half a dozen or so songs that do repeat their middle (with a different lyric), but they needn't trouble us here, and I think that whenever I use this term the reader will understand which section of the song I'm referring to. (You sometimes hear the term 'middle eight', but as Costello's middles range in length from four bars in 'Just a Memory' to thirty-two bars in 'Kid About It' it seems best to drop the 'eight'.)

Some songs end with a coda; usually this is just a repetition of the last line or lines of the chorus, or a slight variation on them, but a few songs introduce new material into the coda, such as 'Beyond Belief'.

Here's an example of how all this works in practice. Anyone sufficiently interested in Costello to be reading this book is very likely to be familiar with 'Oliver's Army', so I shall use this as my sample. The song begins with an instrumental introduction, which is followed by the first verse. The chorus begins as the title phrase is sung, then comes the second verse followed again by the chorus. But this time the chorus is followed by the middle ('Hong Kong . . .'). After this is the third verse, another chorus, and lastly the cries of 'Oh' at the end are the coda. You see? It's all very simple. This lengthy explanation will make things easier later.

A word about the structure of this book. When I first sat down to write it I was faced with the same problem that all critics have to deal with: whether to approach the subject thematically or chronologically. The former is very appealing: chapters on the themes of women, time, politics, puns, melody and so on could make fascinating reading. The great disadvantages of this approach, however, are firstly that it means separating the songs' constituent elements to an alarming degree, so that the discussion of, say, 'This Year's Girl' would be spread around several chapters. Secondly, the reader who was familiar with just a few albums and wanted to read about those only would have problems. So this book is structured chronologically. This makes it very easy to find your way around, but does mean that I've occasionally had to repeat information in different chapters. If anyone reads this book through from beginning to end, I apologise to them for this annoying but unavoidable defect.

Finally, on the subject of my reading of the songs. (I've deliberately shied away from the term 'interpretations' because it sounds as if it involves an over-earnest tooth-combing for arcane hidden meanings, which isn't at all my method.) I have no special qualifications for writing about Costello's songs except that I admire some of them and have listened to them all carefully. Everything I say about them is my own subjective opinion, though I always try to give evidence to support my opinions. My readings are not intended to be the last word on the subject, and I certainly don't claim that they're 'correct' in the sense that they exclude all other possible readings. Many of Costello's songs are good enough to be able to sustain several divergent readings. All I have tried to do is to guide the reader around the songs as clearly and faithfully as possible. My aim is true, too.

1

Getting Taller

In a television programme about his work Costello was once asked, 'Can you tell me about growing up?' He replied, 'I got a lot taller,' which neatly sums it up. There was a time when he was defensive and secretive about his origins, as this evasive reply indicates, and although since then he's become a lot more frank and unashamed his early years are still occasionally the subject of imaginative speculation. For example, some years ago an entirely spurious rumour was going round that he had at one time been a member of the Sex Pistols. For many years he gave very few interviews, and even if he didn't actually encourage such stories he did little or nothing to discourage them, presumably reasoning that they all added to the mystique of his character. The truth, however, is rather more prosaic.

He was born Declan Patrick MacManus (not McManus, as it's often printed) in London on 25 August 1954. Although born a Londoner he has strong Liverpudlian connections, both his parents being Merseysiders by origin. His father was and is a musician; from 1955 until 1969 he was a singer with the Joe Loss Orchestra, a dance band which played for much of this time at the Hammersmith Palais, where Costello himself was destined to later appear. His mother too provided a musical background; for some years she ran the record shop in Selfridges department store. So although it's hard to believe that even had he been the son of tone-deaf philistine stockbrokers music wouldn't have eventually played a big part in his life, as it was his upbringing was auspicious.

Surrounded by music and musicians from an early age, he grew up with a passion that perhaps only such an early exposure can instil. 'I've always been a fan,' he said in an interview much later.

'That's where it all stems from, from this terrific *enthusiasm* for music.' Pop music was especially prominent in his house: dance bands played arrangements of the chart hits of the day, and his father had to learn them, so records were freely available to young Declan. His favourite group as a youngster was the Beatles, demonstrating a lack of originality that fortunately has not lasted through his career. The first record he owned was 'Please Please Me', which he must have bought when he was about nine. Such precocity indicates the depth of his natural response to music.

If music was the inspiration of his early life, then school provided the dull routine. He went to Catholic primary schools (what's that the Jesuits say about 'give me a child until he's seven and I'll give you the man'?), being taught for a time by nuns, then to a secondary modern school in Hounslow in West London. At the age of sixteen he moved with his mother (who had in the meantime separated from her husband) to Liverpool, where he did 'A' levels. He passed English, and this is one of the few bits of biographical information which intrigues me. To pass 'A' level English requires an understanding of literature and its technicalities, and I'd like to find out how much influence he thinks this has had on his work. Is he conscious, for example, of using such devices as antithesis (in which two strongly contrasting words or concepts are opposed, as in 'their hearts are empty when their hands are full' from 'The Comedians'), or is this instinctive? It makes no difference to the quality of the song, or the songwriter, but it would be fascinating to know how his songs are put together. Such a highly literate writer is likely to have at least some literary influences, a handful of which I've tentatively identified.

He left school in about 1972, and although his aspirations were musical had to start looking for a job. Finding one proved to be not too easy (unemployment reached one million at around this time, which seems almost unbelievably low from the perspective of the late eighties but which was a sobering statistic then). Eventually, however, he became a computer operator. This could form the basis of a new after-dinner game: matching public figures with the most absurdly unlikely jobs. The Archbishop of Canterbury as a second-hand car salesman; Mrs Thatcher as an agony aunt; Cilla Black as question-master on *Mastermind* – the possibilities are endless.

But all the time he was computing his chances of finding an opening in the world of rock music. It should be taken as read that through these years his enthusiasm for music remained undimmed. In interviews he has mentioned some of the records that he was listening to at this time, and although this list should be regarded as by no means exhaustive it's an interesting selection. Some singer/songwriters (a term much used in the seventies but now out of fashion) feature on it, such as the rather good Randy Newman and the pitiful James Taylor. There's dance music in the form of the soul *Motown Chartbusters* and the reggae *Tighten Up* compilations. Van Morrison (one of the handful of songwriters whose corpus of albums can stand comparison with Costello's) gets an honourable mention, as do The Band, one of whose singers, Rick Danko, was his favourite vocalist at the time. Dylan too was undoubtedly an influence. It's not too difficult to find traces of all these styles in Costello's work, though he's blended them into an amalgam that's his own.

Just as important as his musical enthusiasms are his antipathies. Glitter rock did not find favour with him, nor did heavy metal, nor American west coast groups such as the Grateful Dead. Perhaps most significantly he strongly disliked groups such as Yes, Emerson, Lake and Palmer, Caravan and Pink Floyd, finding their 'big, heavy messages', (as he described them) pretentious concept albums, pseudo-mystical twaddle and interminable songs far too overblown and self-important. (I'm putting words in his mouth now, but I'm sure he'd agree with the gist of these sentiments.) When he began making records he was very careful to avoid these pitfalls.

Even before he left school he was writing songs and performing them. Many embryonic songwriters have first presented their melodic conceptions to the public in folk clubs, and for a while he performed solo in both Liverpool and London. Later, back in London permanently by this time, he formed a group which eventually came to be called Flip City.

While in the mid-seventies the singles charts were dominated by bubblegum acts such as Gary Glitter and Sweet, and the album charts by the pomp-rockers so frowned on by Costello, the London live music scene had a healthy and flourishing underground in pub-rock. Although difficult to define because by its nature so diverse, pub-rock was characterised by a desire to have a good time rather than make supposedly significant statements, and so a sense of humour and enthusiasm were considered more important than technical virtuosity. Musically rhythm and blues

3

was probably the most widespread influence, and certainly the songs had to be punchy and direct to come across in a crowded, noisy pub. Flip City began to play the pub-rock circuit, and although their success was minimal – there was never any question of their making a record, for example – at least they provided Costello with his first real taste of what it's like to be a rock musician. They even touched the fringes of the big time in 1975 when they supported Dr Feelgood, a pub-rock group who had actually achieved commercial success.

Flip City's repertoire, like that of most other similar groups, was a mixture of cover versions (in deference to the audience's wishes) and self-penned numbers. Costello provided the latter, including one, 'Pay It Back', that appeared on his first album. Although no writer should be judged by his juvenilia it would be interesting to hear what some of those other songs are like. I wonder when his distinctive style and persona first appeared.

Flip City finally split up at the end of 1975. By this time Costello was married with a son, and still tapping away at his computer keyboard by day. But by night he became a solo singer. It was at this stage that he began to shed the name 'Declan MacManus'. The surname seemed a bit of a mouthful, so for stage purposes he changed it to 'Costello', his great-grandmother's name. Styling himself D. P. Costello, he set about trying to make a name for himself in the metaphoric sense too.

At about the same time something new was happening on the British music scene. Costello wasn't the only one who thought that the old excesses of pomp rock should be stamped out. In fact a whole load of people intended to stamp them out by means of a complete set of new excesses. They first began to organise themselves in 1975, had their first successes in 1976 and by 1977 punk had conquered. With the Sex Pistols as its storm-troopers punk took on the whole musical establishment and won. The Pistols, or more precisely their manager Malcolm McLaren, cheerfully collected £175,000 from three record companies in six months, thus becoming a household name when they had released only one single. Punk was suddenly the most talked about and vibrant British musical movement since the Merseybeat boom of the early sixties.

In some respects punk had its roots in pub-rock. Some of its most notable personalities, for example Joe Strummer of the Clash and formerly of the 101ers, had played in pub-rock bands. But where pub-rock had a cheerful refusal to take anything too seriously punk had a furious iconoclasm, sometimes but not always of a radical political nature. Pub-rockers didn't need to be virtuosi on their instruments, but punks positively relished technical limitations. Their mixture of anger, frustration, urban boredom and nihilism was overwhelming, and contributed to the making of some of the most vital singles ever unleashed. Although some punk records are now frankly unlistenable, a few of them still sound just as good more than a decade on. I believe that John Peel still regards the Undertones' 'Teenage Kicks' as his all-time favourite record, a position I'm sometimes inclined to award to the Rezillos' 'I Can't Stand My Baby', or perhaps the Adverts' 'Gary Gilmore's Eyes'.

Costello didn't come straight out of punk, but it plays an important part in his story. Firstly, it confirmed that anger, frustration, nihilism and so on were emotions capable of being expressed by rock music. (I don't mean to suggest that punk was the first rock style to do this, but the pop world of the mid-seventies had largely forgotten this and needed reminding.) Almost certainly Costello was already writing songs embracing such subjects, but punk proved that there was a market for them. Secondly, it encouraged a lot of people to take on the giant record companies by challenging their near-monopoly. I shall return to this in a moment. Thirdly, it spawned the new wave, under whose banner Costello first came to public attention.

'New wave' didn't actually mean much, being more like a convenient label than a real style. I suppose as good a way of explaining it as any is to say that it's a kind of compromise between pub-rock and punk. New wave was on the whole fired by similar emotions as punk, but chose to express them idiosyncratically and sardonically rather than by a directly confrontational approach. Punk loudly proclaimed its desire to burn everything down as soon as possible, while new wave dispensed with the volume and the urgency, replacing them with traditional song structures. In effect, the new wave produced good songs, not just good records, If this doesn't seem to make sense, try to imagine another band making a cover version of the Sex Pistols' 'God Save the Queen', a great record. You can't? Neither can I, because as a song it hardly exists. It's easy, though, to imagine someone covering Costello's songs, because they're substantial in much the same way as songs by Berlin, Porter, Gershwin, Rodgers and Hart,

5

Lennon and McCartney and so on. I use 'new wave' here to mean the revival of a great tradition.

I left D. P. Costello, solo singer, searching for stardom. He adopted the tactic of marching into record company offices, plonking himself down on a seat and plonking away on his guitar in an effort to get a record contract. The only result was that he made himself look a right plonker, and there must be several pavements around London where he's landed after being forcibly ejected. Tired of receiving bruises on his body and dents in his guitar he made a demo tape in 1976 (containing 'Blame It On Cain', and 'Mystery Dance', as well as some other unreleased songs) and started sending it to record companies.

One company he sent it to was Stiff Records. As I've already mentioned, punk, with its anyone-can-have-a-go philosophy, inspired many people to try to break the stranglehold that the big record companies had on the music industry. Previously, unless musicians could get themselves signed up by a major label their chances of getting their music heard were slim. There seemed no reason why this should continue to be so, and small independent labels sprung up as rapidly as estate agents do now. Nowadays we take the 'indies' for granted, but this was a real revolution at the time. Stiff was at the forefront of this revolution – indeed, the first punk single to be available nationally, the Damned's 'New Rose' released in November 1976, was a Stiff record. (As you'll see from the company's name, something of the old pub-rock self-deprecating humour was preserved here, a stiff record being one that doesn't sell.)

The people at Stiff might not have had the subtlest sense of humour (as some of their advertising gimmicks revealed) but at least they had the nous to recognise some good songs when they heard them. They immediately reached for their cheque book and (I've always wanted to be able to write this) the rest is history.

The demo tape which created this enthusiasm consisted simply of Costello singing to the accompaniment of his strummed guitar. Some eight years later this combination was to prove very effective, but the world wasn't yet ready for such a stark presentation. Costello needed a band to back him. The problem was solved by recruiting Clover, a Californian country-rock group, to play on his debut releases. While their good-time approach is slightly out of key with the venom of the songs, they do a good job. In particular we should be grateful to John McFee, the guitarist (who later appeared on Costello's country album *Almost Blue*), whose expertise adds greatly to several songs, especially 'Alison' and 'Sneaky Feelings'. The whole package was produced by the already well-established pop artist, Nick Lowe, thus beginning the long-standing partnership between Lowe and Costello.

The songs from the first album were recorded at the Pathway Studios in Highbury in North London. Costello was still operating his computer at the time, so we're faced with the bizarre image of him simultaneously recording hard cold facts in data banks and impassioned cries from the soul in the studio. Even at this stage of his career he was exhibiting the confidence in his ability and his productivity that was later to become so characteristic. Most of the songs he'd already written were put to one side because they weren't, as he said, 'direct' enough – some of them surfaced, mostly in revised form, on later albums. I can imagine that the people at Stiff were a little apprehensive when they heard this – would the new songs get written to schedule, and would they be any good? They needn't have worried. Costello claims that the bulk of *My Aim Is True* was written in about a fortnight, and I see no reason to disbelieve him. The songs certainly have a spontaneity and immediacy. What's more, they form his most consistent collection to appear before *Get Happy!!* three years later.

One problem remained – his name. Declan MacManus and D. P. Costello are both perfectly reasonable monickers, but somehow don't have the ring of stardom about them. The punk approach to names was to be deliberately outrageous (as in Sid Vicious, Rat Scabies and many others), but such an open challenge to normality seemed inappropriate here. It was obvious that Costello was a subversive but not a firebrand insurrectionist. The answer was to be found in the pub-rock sense of irreverent fun. How about stealing the name of the most revered rocker of all? As Costello later said, 'I thought Elvis was a better name than Jesus, and almost as exclusive.' So Elvis Costello was born. Eerily enough, it seemed as if there were room for only one Elvis in the world, for just a month after the release of *My Aim Is True* Presley died, an involuntary abdication from the kingship of rock that must have left a nasty taste in Costello's mouth at the time. But by then it was too late to think again. Three singles had already been released under his new name, which in retrospect are terrific but received little attention at the time. Despite the singles' failures the album immediately caught the public imagination, selling 11,000 copies in its first three days and eventually reaching number ten in the chart, extremely good for an unknown artist's debut on an independent label. No, Elvis Costello it was now, and he was getting taller all the time.

2

'My Aim Is True'

I first heard *My Aim Is True* at a friend's house in the summer of 1977. I was immediately taken by the unusual vehemence of the music, but what I especially remember is picking up the album sleeve and being a bit puzzled by it. It neither tried to flatter the spectator with seductive images, as most mainstream rock sleeves did, nor did it make any obvious attempt to appeal by being outrageous, as was the current tendency with punk. It was disconcertingly odd; disconcerting because I couldn't at first work out just what was unusual about it.

The photograph on the front showed Costello with legs splayed in the traditional rock guitarists' tough-guy-in-a-shoot-out stance. That much was certainly familiar. But his left leg was knock-kneed and pigeon-toed, making him look pretty seriously constipated. What were we supposed to make of that? His face, too, didn't wear that expression, obligatory for rock musicians' publicity photos, intended to look moodily cocksure but in fact looking sulky and spoiled. He wasn't smiling either. Instead he glared at us, apparently with hostility, through his prominent black-framed glasses, and clutched his guitar as if afraid that someone was going to snatch it. You didn't have to be an expert on body-language to realise that the picture was not exactly welcoming. If you saw this figure coming towards you in the street you might not cross the road to avoid him, but you wouldn't want to stop him to ask the time.

The photograph on the back was rather more comforting. He looked a little more relaxed and approachable, attributes accentuated by his slight resemblance to Buddy Holly. Something was not quite right, though, and it took a while to realise that his head seemed to be disproportionately large, an illusion created

9

perhaps by an unusual camera angle. In contrast to the ominous front photograph, this doll-like appearance gave a sense of child-like vulnerability. But he still looked subtly *wrong*.

Seeing him perform 'Watching the Detectives' on *Top of the Pops* later in 1977, it struck me that because of his gangling, apparently uncoordinated movements and oversized glasses he looked like a demented version of Brains from *Thunderbirds*, the sixties puppet serial. Despite the slogan 'Elvis is king' repeated *ad infinitum* on *My Aim is True*'s sleeve he didn't look at all regal.

I've dwelt on these images at some length, and perhaps endowed them with more significance than they intrinsically possess, because they are important in helping to establish Costello's persona, the stage character he has adopted and used, with many modifications, throughout his career. His physical ungainliness, deliberately exaggerated by the photographs, marks him out as a misfit, a man out of time and place. He's not the cool man of the world many rock singers present themselves as; he's the outsider, observing sardonically from a distance. The Brains-like glasses and head seem to signal an acute intelligence; glasses imply on the one hand short-sightedness, but, paradoxically, on the other hand they also imply perception and vision. The photographs suggest that Costello is someone who stands on the edges of society looking in, and who is far more aware than most of the rest of us of what's going on.

This persona is a variant of a long-established figure, dating back at least as far as the jester of medieval and earlier times: regarded by most people as not quite normal, perhaps socially inept, possibly even the butt of ridicule, and so forced to live on his wits, alert, thoughtful, and capable of drawing attention to uncomfortable truths. Other modern versions of this figure are numerous. To give just two contrasting examples, there's the tragic Piggy in William Golding's novel *Lord of the Flies*, and in a lighter vein the character played by Woody Allen in many of his films, (*Love and Death*, for example). It's not so common, though, for rock musicians to adopt this pose, and it's worth asking why Costello (and of course whoever else had a hand in the sleeve) chose this particular image.

It owes something to the punk movement, which revitalised the tradition of anger and rebellion in the promotion of rock, but almost always in a far more overt and violent manner than Costello's relatively understated expression of discontent. To see

10

the truth of this statement you only have to compare the defiant grotesqueries of the Sex Pistols' public image, or the surly aggressiveness of the Clash's, with Costello's. Punks, with their deliberately outrageous appearance and attitudes, obviously intended to challenge and shock, but Costello, in his choice of image as in most other things he does, was subtler.

No doubt it was originally suggested by his 'real' character, with which it presumably has some similarities, but more important was the (as it's turned out, correct) guess that a large number of people would respond to and identify with this image. Everyone who'd ever found themselves in the kitchen at a party when everyone else was apparently having a whale of a time in the rest of the house, everyone who'd at some time felt that the world was all wrong but that spraying graffiti on walls wasn't much of a solution, recognised in Costello's persona something of themselves. Almost everyone must feel a bit like this occasionally, no one is immune from insecurity and doubt, and the sleeve of *My Aim Is True* proclaims that here is a spokesman for such feelings. Although he looks as if he's going to stutter, again like Brains, in fact the record is a damburst of torrential eloquence.

The lyrics of almost all Costello's songs can be provisionally divided into two categories: they are either about personal relationships, or they deal with public and what can be called, broadly speaking, political issues. As if to draw attention to this fact and to state the themes that are to be the subject of this and the next nine albums, the first two songs on *My Aim Is True* are examples of these two types, 'Welcome to the Working Week' being a public song and 'Miracle Man' personal.

Most of Costello's songs are aflame with rage and bitterness: in 'Welcome to the Working Week' the narrator burns while financiers fiddle their tax returns, for it deals with the ruthlessness of the business world which, according to Costello, has most of us in its grasp. The first line is apparently addressed to a girl who has achieved some sort of success by having her pin-up picture printed in the tabloid press, where it is leered at and perhaps masturbated over. The second verse introduces the theme of the savagery that he detects under the civilised surface of life. Some people have to 'kill to survive', though even stabbing people in the back does not guarantee a large income or a leisured life. Only a fortunate few arrive at their 'big day', such as the pin-up girl, and her success is bound by its nature to be short-lived. The song's middle ('I hear you saying . . .'), however, implies that there is a group of people whose success is longer-lasting. Someone claims that 'the city's all right', and while 'city' could simply mean a large town, *the* city suggests the world of big business and high finance, where newspaper-owners who profit from printing pictures of topless girls are to be found. The success they allow her to have is merely illusory, because being a figure in the furtive fantasies of fetishists is demeaning, and anyway it won't be long before she's displaced by younger models. In short, they exploit her.

The song is addressed to 'you', which primarily refers to the girl, but when listening to Costello's songs we must be ready to accept rapidly changing view-points and perspectives. The pronoun 'you' can be taken as referring not only to the girl, but also to the listener and the world at large. Thus the song ironically welcomes us all to the 'working week', and the girl becomes a symbol of everyone who is manipulated by those more powerful than themselves, (though like all good symbols it works on a literal level too). We are like her, Costello claims, because we are trapped into working for people who cynically use us for their own ends.

This sense of being ensnared and exploited fills the narrator with impotent fury. He is powerless because if the powerful knew about his secret resentment they'd 'bury [him] alive' – a horrifying way of expressing the mercilessness of the powerful when dealing with those who don't toe the line. Consequently he is 'like a juggler running out of hands', a neat image of not being in control of one's own destiny, of being unable to cope with the ringmaster's dictations.

The song sketches a world in which a few profit from the failure of the many and against which it is useless to protest. There is nothing original in Costello's analysis of society – his ideas, as opposed to his expression of them, are fairly commonplace. What makes them worth listening to is the immediacy he gives them, so that we are shocked into considering them with new intensity. He achieves this partly by using as his central image something with which we're all familiar, the pin-up girl, and so bringing the ideas close to home. We are emotionally convinced far more effectively than we would be by, say, statistics supporting his argument. Similarly, by giving the song a first person narrator ('I') with whom we can identify and sympathise he invites us to share his indignation. All this sounds rather earnest, so let's not forget that 'Welcome to the Working Week' is also a gutsy rock song that evokes feelings of frustration while at the same time providing some release from them through its trenchant exhilaration.

'Miracle Man', a personal song, is in its way just as cynical and bitter, but instead of dealing with the relationships between the various sections of society it deals with the relationship between one man and one woman. And a very unsatisfactory relationship it appears to be. She treats him with sneering contempt, finding fault with everything he does. She is portrayed as domineering in an almost sado-masochistic way, for she has a 'ten-inch bamboo cigarette holder' and wears 'black patent leather gloves' like something from a Berlin brothel, though there's an element of the comically absurd in this too.

Here Costello's persona is that of the luckless lover, cursed by a disdainful woman. In the previous song he portrays himself as an economic failure, while here another kind of failure is presented, the inability to sustain a satisfactory relationship. The sound of the song drips resentment and anger, his voice brims with acrimony. This persona, and the figure of the woman who requires her men to humble themselves by 'crawling round on all fours', is to crop up over and over again on the succeeding albums.

'No Dancing' is also about a personal relationship, but differs from all the other *My Aim Is True* songs because the narrator does not appear to be involved in the song's events. Instead he appears only in the opening verse, but observes the behaviour of the lovers throughout the song. This device creates a curious voyeuristic effect, as if Costello were ghoulishly drawn to watching the grisly details of the affair unfold, as passers-by become spectators of car crashes.

The opening lines leave us in no doubt that the woman is as heartless as the one in 'Miracle Man', and that such behaviour is not rare. She has 'made a fool' of the man, as women have done countless times before. Later in the song the man says that he has to continually 'bow' to her. Women are the real holders of power in relationships, and consequently have to be treated like haughty queens. But in return they are not gracious or loyal, but are fickle and withdraw their favours at whim.

Earlier writers have noted that dancing on *My Aim Is True* is a metaphor for sex, and this is certainly true as far as it goes. To say that there will be 'no dancing' on a simple level means that they are not going to make love. However, there are also deeper implications. Dancing is an archetypal symbol, an idea that means something to our subconscious mind, expressing the creation of order and the communal celebration of harmony. This is why weddings, for example, traditionally involve some form of dancing. There is a significant tradition of rock songs that utilise dancing for this purpose, usually in the form of a celebration of the togetherness of teenagers, for example 'At the Hop' and 'Dancing in the Street'. To state that there is 'no dancing' is thus an exact negation of order and harmony: Costello implies that the world is chaotic and full of enmity. Seen in this light the song becomes more than a whinge about the difficulty of obtaining a decent bonk, and lines such as 'somebody has to cry' take on new significance. If we think back to Costello's persona in the previous songs we can see that he is developing the figure of the outsider adrift in an orderless world, where suffering seems to be the only constant.

From *Get Happy!!* onwards unexpected key changes, in which the harmonic foundations of a song suddenly shift, become almost commonplace, but, as one would expect from a songwriter still learning his trade, such sophisticated musical devices are much rarer in this early period. 'No Dancing' is in the key of D major, but the middle ('He's getting down . . .') suddenly jolts into D minor, which, like all minor keys, is potentially mournful or even, as in this case, horror-stricken. This abrupt change of key is literally as well as metaphorically disharmonious, the ear expecting sharp Fs and Cs, hearing instead naturals and flat Bs, and is as disturbing as feeling the foundations of a building being shaken by an earthquake. The coda (the repetitions of 'There's gonna be . . .') also has an unsettling change of key, and thus enforces Costello's sense of being out of place with apparently out of place notes. The unusually subtle music ensures that 'No Dancing' is one of the album's best songs.

'Blame It On Cain' returns to the public territory of 'Welcome to the Working Week', though while the opening song attacks simply 'the city' here Costello is slightly more specific. 'Government burglars' take his money, presumably in the form of taxes, and 'the man with the tickertape' conspires to do the same. We are also given Costello's thoughts on how we are persuaded to part with our cash. Even when someone succeeds in acquiring some

14

they can't hold on to it for long, because 'the radio, that heaven, will be wired to your purse'. The radio, according to the song, has such a powerful influence that it seems as if its exhortations to spend go straight to our wallets, bypassing our brains. The choice of the word 'wired' is especially effective here, because it insinuates that we are like robots, programmed to respond to stimuli. The signal 'Buy!' is cabled to us, and our Pavlovian reaction is to rush out to get the latest obsolescent consumer 'durable' in a doomed attempt to reach the promised 'heaven'.

The chorus is like that of 'No Dancing' in that it enlarges the implication of the song. The verses are about financial restrictions and the consequent loss of freedom, but the chorus makes no mention of this, referring instead only to 'it', which should be blamed on Cain, not the narrator. In the Bible Cain is, of course, the first murderer, and can therefore be accused of beginning man's deliberate cruelty to man, of which the various imprisonings in the verses are examples. But because the chorus refers only to 'it' we can take this as including all the other dissatisfactions of life too, such as those evoked by the album's other songs. At the end of the second verse he states 'you're not satisfied', implying that the world is fundamentally frustrating. This is nobody's fault, even the men with the tickertape cannot be blamed for it. It is an inescapable fact that cannot be pinned down on anyone and so cannot be corrected. All that can be done is to let off steam to no material purpose, to find 'somebody to burn' as a scapegoat. The sense of impotence is almost unbearable, and is most evident in the virtually shouted last line of the last verse: 'how much longer?' This is a despairing question because the song gives no hint that anything is ever going to change.

The feeling of tensely waiting for something that's not going to arrive is recreated by the music, by means of a device found quite frequently on Costello's early albums, that of extended verses. The first verse is twelve bars long, which creates in the listener the expectation that the other verses will be of the same length. In fact the second is sixteen bars long and the third seventeen, which means that the listener is left hanging, wondering when the chorus is going to arrive, almost physically gripped by the desire for a satisfactory conclusion.

'Alison' is probably the album's best-known song, and rightly so, for, if it makes any sense to speak of pop songs lasting two minutes as masterpieces, it is Costello's earliest masterpiece. The

15

beautiful melody, aching with longing and tenderness, is one of the few that could stand by itself without the support of the lyrics. All the other songs on the album are angry and bitter, and while these emotions are not entirely absent from 'Alison' – a Costello song without them would be like Hamlet without Bach's Air on a G string – they are muted, and gentler feelings take the ascendancy. It is significant, however, that the album's only tender song is about a past rather than a present relationship – indeed, it is arguable that Costello has written no unambiguously happy love songs, a rare feat for a major songwriter.

The narrator meets Alison, with whom he has some time ago had a romance, and who is now married to someone else. She bears some similarity to the woman in 'Miracle Man' because she is 'not impressed' with the narrator, but this does not prevent him regretting their separation. His feelings about her marriage are marvellously expressed in the line 'I heard you let that little friend of mine take off your party dress'. His description of her husband is slyly contemptuous, and it is hinted that he has corrupted her innocence, since 'party dress' as a description of clothing is often associated with young girls. He promises not to 'get too sentimental' and cause an embarrassing scene, as would 'those other sticky Valentines'. This phrase is just right in the context, suggesting adolescent sickly sweet emotions and precocious sexuality, combining disgust with a longing for it all to be as simple as that for him.

The chorus is heart-stoppingly poignant. The fact that she is named, unlike the women in almost all of Costello's other songs, is in itself affecting. The sustained note on the syllable 'Al', followed by the jerky rhythm of 'I know this world' and the painfully rising phrase of 'is killing you', contrasts her apparent calm with his confusion and awkwardness. The song ends with quiet assertions of sincerity, and the introspective doodles of the guitar drift it to a suitably wistful conclusion.

The first five songs are all fraught with tension and are exhausting to listen to, so it is appropriate that side one should end with 'Sneaky Feelings', which is somewhat lighter in mood. The subject matter, a distintegrating relationship, is in itself not exactly easy listening, but the treatment of it, and especially the music, is almost perky.

It begins with a sprightly syncopated guitar riff which is comically at odds with the opening lines. These evoke a nightmare

16

vision of everyone assuming that their partner will be unfaithful, and so trying to gain the upper hand by being themselves unfaithful first. He notes with wry humour that dreaming about his lover is 'not so much fun' as knowing her in reality, but at least 'it's safer that way'. The world is a hostile and dangerous place.

The 'sneaky feelings' are all the longings we have for the unattainable, feelings which will only cause suffering and so must be suppressed. Though it has to be said that Costello has not made a very determined effort to disguise his dissatisfactions so far on the album. He would like to 'get right through' these feelings, not be so haunted by them, but recognises that he has 'still got a long way to go'. Indeed, it is not until *Trust* at the earliest that he begins to show any convincing signs of having done so.

A cursory hearing suggests that '(The Angels Wanna Wear My) Red Shoes' is simply another personal song about a disintegrating relationship. The first verse (though as the song begins, untypically, with the chorus the verse does not arrive until the twenty-fifth bar) is set in some kind of dance hall, where Costello's persona watches his lover as she is 'dancing away', (in itself a telling phrase, for at first sight the adverb just strengthens the verb, but later we realise that she is dancing *away* from him). Thinking back to the deeper implications of dancing, we see that she is enjoying the social harmony from which he is excluded. Their relationship has been 'fractured', a painfully physical way of describing its breakdown. What's more she has caused him to be 'punctured'. Again a woman is portrayed as heartless and potentially violent, and nowhere is this better shown than in the tearful but farcically indignant couplet

I said, 'I'm so happy I could die,'
She said, 'Drop dead', then left with another guy.

Despite the anguish of these lines I can't help grinning with delight when I hear them, so rueful is his self-mockery and so neat her response. We can imagine Costello, the eternal loser, blinking bewilderedly behind his National Health specs.

The woman is not portrayed throughout the song just as a persecutor of men, but as a victim of them too. In the middle ('Oh, I know that she's . . .') she is 'disgusted' and 'feeling so abused' because 'she gets tired of the lust'. For once Costello

17

acknowledges that women as well as men have to endure hardships, though this point is almost undercut by the backing vocals
interpolating 'Oh, that's too bad' in a tone of voice dangerously
close to sarcasm. Nevertheless, 'Red Shoes' is a rare example of
a song which expresses some sympathy for women.

So far this discussion has taken no account of the chorus (which
begins and ends the song), or the title. The 'red shoes' themselves
are on a superficial level a symbol of elegance, or perhaps flam-
boyance; red shoes have been used to this effect in other rock
songs, such as David Bowie's 'Let's Dance', and there is a parallel
instance in Carl Perkins' 'Blue Suede Shoes'. However, if we look
more closely at the symbolism traditionally associated with red
and with shoes a much more complex and interesting interpretation begins to emerge. Red, largely because it is the colour of
blood, is a symbol of life, passion, vitality, masculinity and other
related concepts. Shoes, perhaps surprisingly, are symbolically
charged with significance. One of their main connotations is that
of freedom, probably because in the past children went barefoot
in certain societies, so the wearing of shoes became associated
with authority and adulthood. Slaves too were denied shoes while
their masters wore them, so again shoes came to signify the power
to control one's own destiny, in other words freedom. Over the
centuries this association of shoes and freedom has become part
of mankind's collective memory, so when Costello says that the
angels want to wear his red shoes he is implying, perhaps half-
unconsciously, that the forces which control us, such as that of
malignant fate (sarcastically addressed as 'angels'), are trying to
take away from him his vigour and his freedom. Our angry Jung
man portrays the universe as malevolent and untrustworthy,
scheming to steal his individuality.

'(The Angels Wanna Wear My) Red Shoes' is one of Costello's
most multi-layered songs – further symbological readings are
available to anyone willing to look carefully enough. One route
of investigation would be to compare the song to Hans Andersen's
extraordinary fairy tale 'The Red Shoes', and another would be
to pursue the symbolic connection between shoes and the female
genitals (which arises because of the similarity of their shapes).
Having read this you'll never be able to put on your trainers so
innocently again.

The complexities of the song do not end there. The angels'
'wings have got rusted' and presumably they want his red shoes,

18

his youthful energy, in order to reverse this ageing process. In return he 'won't get any older', he will be given eternal youth. This is, however, a bad bargain, a con-trick, because as we've already seen, what they are taking *is*, in effect, his youth. He realises this himself in the middle where he admits that the angels have 'stolen' his red shoes. His lover rejects him for, among other reasons, being too old, so clearly the angels have duped him.

This at last brings us to what I regard as the song's central concern: time. *My Aim Is True* has already dealt with various sources of dissatisfaction, and the remaining songs present us with more. One of the most enraging features of reality is time – its progress is merciless, constantly taking us closer to the helplessness of old age and the nullity of death. To escape 'the iniquity of oblivion' (to use Sir Thomas Browne's superb phrase) is probably one of mankind's oldest and most deep-seated desires. 'Red Shoes' dramatises this desire and its inevitable futility, a theme to which several subsequent songs return.

'Less Than Zero' is the most openly political song on the album. In the opening line Costello invokes 'Mister Oswald' which to English listeners at least will call to mind Oswald Mosley, leader of the British Union of Fascists in the 1930s. He has a 'swastika tattoo', which links him both with the crimes of the Nazis and with more modern fascists, such as National Front skinheads. Costello obliquely accuses him of an ingenious assortment of misdeeds: sadism, brutality, probably homosexual rape and possibly incest, dealing in pornographic videos and straightforward murder. One wonders how he found the time to run a party too, but of course the historical Mosley (who was still alive when the song was written) is not seriously being accused of these specific crimes, but he becomes in the song a symbol of corruption and decadence. It does not take much imagination to suspect that, in Costello's eyes, the song's version of Mosely is only an extreme example of the men with the tickertape, who also treat people with amoral indifference. The city might not actually rape or murder people but metaphorically, Costello implies, it does. This idea comes very close to being explicit when a murder is committed, presumably by Mister Oswald, but he is complacent because he has 'an understanding with the law'. The judiciary turns a blind eye, presumably because it is secretly sympathetic to Mosley. Thus the whole of the establishment is implicated in the evils he is accused of.

19

Typically, the chorus adds a new dimension to the song. 'Welcome to the Working Week' and 'Blame It On Cain' have already hinted at the power of the media, but 'Less Than Zero' is more specific. 'Turn up the TV, no one listening will suspect' suggests that one of the functions of the media is to conceal the corruption of the establishment from its victims, to blunt the senses of the viewers with escapist programmes in order to discourage them from thinking about what's happening in the real world. Turning up the volume on the television drowns the screams as Mister Oswald sends his victims off to die.

Previous songs have established that the world is random, so it comes as no surprise that 'everything means less than zero' to Costello. Once again we are left with the impression that there is no justice, that the powerful can do as they like and get away with it. 'Less Than Zero' peers into the void, hoping to discover the meaning or purpose of life, the eschatological ends, but finds instead only *Coronation Street*.

'Mystery Dance' continues the theme of dancing, which again is a metaphor for sex and happiness. It is specifically about people's first experiences of sex, when things rarely go as one is lead to believe they will. The subject is treated with great humour, the first joke being the musical style. It is highly reminiscent of 1950s rock and roll ('Jailhouse Rock' is the main prototype), a genre of ostentatious virility: it's difficult to imagine the original Elvis singing about not knowing what to do with his plonker. To have set the words to such inappropriate music is delightful.

The second verse is a rueful description of what happened, or didn't happen, 'when the lights went out'. Both he and she tried to appear confident and assumed that the other was experienced in such matters, but in fact they 'didn't know how to do it'. Rock singers are more often prone to imply or even announce that they are good in bed, so it's refreshing to find one singing about sexual ineptitude. Memories of adolescent fumblings and bumblings will no doubt be evoked in many listeners.

Sex is a 'mystery dance' because the narrator is puzzled by it, but the remarks on the significance of dance in 'No Dancing' also apply here. He is 'still mystified' and 'not satisfied' – the latter phrase is repeated over and over again to make sure we've got the point. The world is as bafflingly uncontrollable and frustrating as ever, and to cap it all he has angst in his pants.

'Pay It Back' has some similarities with other songs about

personal relationships. Costello implies, for example, that marriage is 'being trapped'. In subsequent songs one of his characteristic devices is to make what at first seems a comforting statement but then undercut it, and this is evident when he states that he loves her, but then adds laconically 'I don't expect that will last'. Even love is eroded by time.

More importantly, 'Pay It Back' has affinities with the public songs 'Welcome to the Working Week' and 'Blame It On Cain'. The last couplet of the last verse in some ways sums up the album:

They told me everything was guaranteed;
Somebody somewhere must've lied to me.

The media generally imply that life is uncomplicated and pleasurable, with labour-saving gadgets in the kitchen, undemanding newspapers and television programmes in the sitting room and simple sex in the bedroom, all with their easy-to-follow instruction manuals. The narrator discovers that life is far more complex and disturbing than he's been told, and the last line of the last couplet is sung with real anguish as he realises that he's been betrayed and sold short by the consumer con-trick. He's not even sure who to blame, just 'somebody somewhere'.

In many ways *My Aim Is True* is a very typical Elvis Costello album, and one of its characteristics is that although it starts extremely well it falls off badly towards the end. The last two songs are probably the weakest, 'I'm Not Angry' being too much like a self-parody and 'Waiting for the End of the World' being too far removed from the everyday world which is Costello's most fruitful territory. What's more, both songs feature lurid and melodramatic guitar which sounds draped with studs and chains, as if it's escaped from a heavy metal album being recorded in an adjacent studio.

'I'm Not Angry' is the most open expression on the album of disgust for women and sex. As before the narrator is jealous and contemptuous of his sexual rival, putting him down as a 'joker'. He is humiliated by being rejected, but claims in the chorus that he is 'not angry', a strange statement to come from a card-carrying angry young man. In fact, of course, the vehemence of his denial shows his claim to be simply tearful bravado, a sad attempt to hide from himself and the listener how deeply he has been hurt and his pride wounded.

21

Sex is rarely if ever presented by Costello as joyful, and in this song it is seen as disgusting and demeaning. What would be described by most people as ecstatic cries are called 'the stutter of ignition', making them sound mechanical and inhuman. The woman is said to be 'smiling with [her] legs', a revolting image, full of contempt for her sexuality. Although the antics of the lovers are hurtful to the narrator he takes a rather prurient interest in them. He is doing his best to see as much as he can, matching their dirty deeds with his dirty raincoat.

'Waiting for the End of the World' differs from most of the other songs because it treats its subject matter with sardonic detachment. It is a surrealistic narrative of a rather Dylanesque nature ('Motorpsycho Nightmare' and 'Bob Dylan's 115th Dream' come to mind as possible influences), a form Costello rarely attempted again. The events of the song take place during a train journey, which is presumably a symbol of life, during which there are a number of disturbing occurrences. The occupants of the carriage seem to resent the power of 'the man from the television' and so will 'probably pull his hands off'. This gruesome image is followed by a power failure which results in their being 'stuck in the tunnel where no lights shine', a not especially subtle symbol of moral sterility. In the chorus Costello 'sincerely hope[s]' that the world is going to come to an end, because the Second Coming of Christ is the only thing that could be expected to make any improvement to such a godforsaken place. He dryly remarks that God 'really started something' when He created the world.

In the second verse there is an enjoyable portrait of, apparently, a hopelessly dated hippy, who claims to 'know where it's at', but his idea of perfection combines the tacky with the dreamily vague: 'he'd like to go to Spain or somewhere like that'. Perhaps he represents our desire to escape from the grim world in which we live, and the impossibility of doing so.

In 'Waiting for the End of the World' Costello's persona supposes that God has blithely, or perhaps even maliciously, created the universe but then allowed it to be manipulated by whoever manages to seize power. Thus it lacks both order and justice. Costello seems to believe that it is in the cynical hands of the men with the tickertape and those responsible for the various branches of the media. The urgency of *My Aim Is True*, as its title proclaims, derives from his passionate desire to draw attention to this thesis, because he evidently thinks that many people don't realise what's happening. In 'Welcome to the Working Week' he claims that 'you never even bother to look' at the real world, (as opposed to seeing it through the media's rosy camera lenses). By now we realise that 'you' often refers not only to the song's immediate addressee but to us, the listeners. Instead of looking we 'spend all [our] money getting so convinced', which suggests that we are so intent on keeping up with the Joneses, revelling in materialism, that self-abuse has blinded us.

This case is argued with missionary fervour, and though it could be said that Costello's moral stance sometimes comes dangerously close to self-righteousness (and his downtrodden persona to self-pity), agree with his views or not, it must be admitted that the songs create a consistent world-view and make gripping listening.

A fairly common theme of literature is that although the world is a harsh and cruel place at least individuals can find solace in love. *My Aim Is True* denies even this. All the relationships between men and women are in various ways unsatisfactory, and on the whole Costello places the blame for this on the woman, who is usually portrayed as fickle, bitchy and domineering. This has lead to his being accused of misogyny, a charge to which I shall return later. A partial answer to this accusation is that he is chiefly concerned with presenting a pessimistic view of life, and his portrayal of women contributes to this. It could be said that by using women as images of the intractability of life he is simply following a centuries-old tradition. In Greek mythology the Furies or Fates, the avenging deities who punish and torment mankind, are female and their attributes – being fickle, bitchy and domineering – are the same as those given by Costello to women. Throughout his work women are loved, or at least desired, but also feared, and following the developments of this theme is one of the fascinations of tracing his career.

So far I have by and large maintained that the two categories of songs, the personal and the public, are separate. To do so makes the discussion simpler, but it is really an over-simplification, because the two are intermingled and can even be regarded as two approaches to the same end. So, for example, the personal song 'No Dancing' is not only about the failure of one relationship, but about the inevitable eventual failure of all attempts to create harmony, and in 'Miracle Man' the woman behaves very like the authority figures in the public songs. Conversely, some of

23

the public songs are not only about the ruthlessness of the business world but also the unsatisfactory nature of personal relationships. The main subject of *My Aim Is True* is the unaccommodating nature of the world, and this is dealt with in two main ways — the personal songs as the microcosm, and the public as the macrocosm. Although I shall continue, for the sake of convenience, to make reference to these categories, this qualification should always be borne in mind.

Listening to the lyrics is a mostly harrowing experience. There are a few flashes of humour, a fair amount of wit and only the tiniest tendrils of tenderness, but otherwise the nihilistic picture is that of the innocent abroad in a bafflingly cruel world, where all attempts to find a place for oneself are frustrated by women and authority. The barbarity is reflected by frequent references to violence, injury and death — there are over twenty, including two, disturbingly, to premature burial. The listener is not even allowed the luxury of being able to view the narrator's sufferings from a comfortable distance, because all the songs are in the first person and Costello's very direct vocal delivery means that it is impossible to listen to the album with disinterest — he continually grabs us by the shirt front and harangues us, and we are sucked into the vortex to participate imaginatively.

The music, too, ensures that we keep listening. There are some genuine felicities of musical expression, though on the whole the compositions and performances exhibit solid workmanship rather than outstanding brilliance. In general the musicians seem to be enjoying themselves and the producer, Nick Lowe, keeps everything moving with the minimum of fancy filigree. This is fine, but what really grips is Costello's voice, which is so wonderfully suited to the sort of song he writes that I'm almost convinced that there must be a presiding deity ordaining such things, despite Costello's best efforts to convince me otherwise. If the universe were truly random then Sod's Law would probably have prevailed and the songwriter Costello would have ended up with the equally wonderful but entirely unsuitable voice of Frank Sinatra or Peter Pears. Thankfully, the voice that he has ended up with is the perfect vehicle for expressing anger, disgust and bewilderment. His voice is often at odds with the rather relaxed musical backing, but this anomaly only heightens his performance by emphasising every near-sob, scream and sneer. I include the qualifying 'near' because this is by no means a no-holds-barred primal scream session, but a disciplined display of vocal control. To take an example almost at random, listen to the way his voice almost, but not quite, cracks with despair in the phrase 'white lies' in 'Sneaky Feelings'. *My Aim Is True* is a magnificently measured cry of rage; there are plenty of rough edges, but the album remains a remarkably assured achievement for someone only twenty-two years old.

1977 saw the release of two more songs by Costello, one an enjoyable though fairly lightweight piece, the other one of his most enduring creations. 'Radio Sweetheart', the B-side of his first single, 'Less Than Zero', is tinged with country-rock and takes as its theme the separation of the narrator from his 'sweetheart', though we aren't told why they've parted, possibly because their families disapprove of the affair. If so, this is a rare example of the woman not being to blame for the relationship's failure. The narrator hopes that his girlfriend will remain faithful despite the pressures of the mercenary world, but the last verse ends on a despairing note, 'you and I, we have been sold', implying that they stand no chance. Nevertheless, 'Radio Sweetheart' is one of the rosier songs of this period, because at least she is his 'sweetheart', and the invigorating modulation from G major to E major at the beginning of the chorus at least provides a temporary feeling of uplift.

The other 1977 song, 'Watching the Detectives', uses as its central image a television series (presumably American) about the police. The mood is set by the sinister minor key introduction, into which Costello's serpentine guitar insinuates itself. The first verse describes the synthetic, too-perfect beauty of the glamorous women who appear in such programmes, and also of the woman who is watching the television. They are 'nice girls', the sarcasm of this becoming evident in the next phrase where he describes them as 'cellophane shrink-wrapped', like supermarket commodities.

In the chorus the emphasis shifts from the women on the screen to the woman in the room. She appears to be oblivious to her lover's pleas; she is too involved in the fantasy world of 'watching the detectives', and reserves her affection for the make-believe policeman: ' "Ooh, he's so cute!" ' However, the world as depicted on the screen is unsubtly brutal: 'they shoot, shoot, shoot, shoot', which Costello sings to a frighteningly disjointed rhythm on a phrase of rising intonation and horror, one of the

25

most apocalyptic moments in any of his songs. The hero of the programme is beaten up and she is moved to tears, but she shows no emotion for her lover or indeed anything in reality. Thus she is like the detective who 'can't be wounded 'cause he's got no heart'. This statement works on two levels: firstly because he is not real but only a character in a TV series and so the violence is staged and hurts no one, but secondly, and more importantly, because the character is heartless in the sense of lacking compassion. He is a macho dispenser of 'instant justice' who shoots crooks with as much emotion as if he were firing at targets in a rifle range.

Until the second verse the song is in the third person, but a first person narrator mysteriously appears, who is aghast at the horrors being enacted for his entertainment on the television screen. The woman, on the other hand, is 'filing her nails' while watching a gruesome hunt for a murder victim's body. The picture this conjures up of her vacuous indifference to human suffering makes this one of Costello's best lines. The last verse suggests that the narrator and the listener cannot complacently watch and assume that they are above all this. Fiction and reality are no longer separate but become mingled, as the TV detectives come to tap on the narrator's window. He becomes aware that he is a part of their world, because the real world is just as amoral and brutal as the programme. We are all living in a world where parents swap their children for cars, as in 'Less Than Zero'. Life is like a brash and barbaric American cop drama.

Like much good literature 'Watching the Detectives' expresses an abstract and complex idea by means of a concrete and simple image. Costello has hit upon an image at once familiar to everyone likely to hear the song and yet which is flexible and powerful enough to bear the weight of meaning placed upon it. The song appears in his live performances more frequently than most songs dating from the 1970s, its reggae-influenced rhythms generally assuring that it is one of the highlights of his shows. It's interesting to compare the brooding, intense original recording with later live versions, for example the one on the EP given away with early copies of *Armed Forces*. This is much faster than the original, more furious and fiery. This difference is partly due to the arrival of Costello's new backing group, the Attractions, who first appeared (apart from some live performances released as B-sides) on his follow-up album, *This Year's Model*.

3

'This Year's Model'

When *My Aim Is True* became a commercial success Costello decided to form a band to back him on a permanent basis. The result was the Attractions, who, as they have since performed with Costello on the great majority of his recordings, (the only important exception being most of *King Of America*), and have undoubtedly contributed a great deal to the success of his music, deserve some attention. The Attractions consist of Bruce Thomas, a bassist whose playing is exceptionally melodic and who appeared on several folk-rockish albums in the early seventies; Pete Thomas (no relation), a powerful and inventive drummer previously of pub-rockers Chilli Willi and the Red Hot Peppers; and Steve Nieve, a dexterous and versatile keyboard player with, amazingly, no pop pedigree at all, who trained at the Royal College of Music. Together with Costello's rudimentary but passionate guitar they form a band capable of making even mediocre music listenable and of giving Costello's greatest songs an enthralling sense of intensity and immediacy.

It is worth comparing the original version of 'Miracle Man' with the version that appears on the *Live Stiffs* album (recorded at a concert given by musicians signed to the Stiff record label) to get some idea of the Attractions' musical influence. The earlier recording is somewhat laid-back, the emotion depending mostly on the lyric and Costello's vocal delivery, while the later one is much more impassioned, hinting at violent feelings barely kept in check – so much so, indeed, that Costello, after the first few lines, hardly feels the need to exert himself and sings in a rather matter-of-fact manner. Another crucial difference is that the main melodic instrument is no longer the guitar, Nieve's keyboards having taken over that role, producing, with Costello's vocals, one of the most consistently entertaining double-acts in rock music. There is scarcely a single song in which the piano, organ or synthesizer does not key up the appropriate atmosphere or mingle in fascinating rhythms and counter-melodies.

Incidentally, although it strictly speaking falls outside the scope of this book, another song on *Live Stiffs* is notable. This is Burt Bacharach and Hal David's 'I Just Don't Know What To Do With Myself', the first cover version recorded by Costello. It is a potentially saccharine little piece with banal lyrics (though the tune is rather fine) which Costello and the Attractions treat entirely seriously. Yet the effect is exquisite: adolescent anguish at failed romance is touchingly conveyed. The simply maudlin is avoided, such is the commitment of the performance (especially the lugubriously fluid bass) which convinces us of the reality of the emotions.

It's not difficult to see why Costello chose 'I Just Don't Know What To Do With Myself', for its theme — boy loses girl but wants her back — is the theme of several of his own songs of this period, (as well as of thousands of other popular songs). However, Hal David's lyric, while possessing a certain unsophisticated charm, is not much more than an assemblage of near-clichés, a fact that becomes obvious when one compares it with Costello's unorthodox variations on the same theme, for example the song that opens *This Year's Model*, 'No Action'.

The first twist in 'No Action' is that in the opening verse, far from wanting his lover back, the narrator's contempt for her is rivalled only by his disgust at the thought of kissing or touching her. The first line is sung unaccompanied, and Costello intones it as if a sneer is contorting his whole face. The Attractions then erupt in an outburst of almost demonic fury — an extremely effective method of grabbing the listener's attention at the start of an album. He likens holding her to holding the telephone, an unflattering comparison to say the least. She is as unarousing and unresponsive as a piece of plastic, and consequently there's 'no action' in their relationship. One of the frustrations expressed on *My Aim Is True* is the feeling that it is impossible to make anything happen or change anything, so perhaps this chorus, as well as complaining about her supposed frigidity, is also a cry of languid world-weariness.

The chorus is his most ambitious piece of vocal multi-tracking so far, so that we hear what amounts to virtually a choir of

Costellos, all bitterly lamenting their imprisonment in ennui. (Just for a moment I am confronted by the awful and awesome vision of a horde of deranged Buddy Holly clones swarming onto a concert platform intent on doing terminal violence to the *Messiah* or the *Symphony of a Thousand*. But thankfully the vision fades.)

In the second verse, however, Costello changes his tune, and the first signs of cracks in his carefully contrived mask appear. He thinks back to the times they spent together – as we've seen in 'Alison', tenderness is possible only in retrospect, impossible to achieve in the present, so the only way to satisfy the need for love is to nostalgically long for an idealised past. 'Knowing you're with him is driving me crazy' is just as tearful and clichéd as anything in David's lyric, but what saves Costello's line from inanity is the frenzy of the music, once again making effective use of the extended verse (as in 'Blame It On Cain') which compels us to feel the power of the metaphor as if we'd never before heard the much over-used phrase 'it's driving me crazy'. So the triumphantly independent Costello of the first verse quickly proves to be a sham, and he stands revealed as just as bewildered and vulnerable as on *My Aim Is True*.

'No Action' is also interesting as it's the earliest example of a Costello song to use what I shall call thematic punning, by which I mean incorporating into a song several references to a theme which is not the song's true subject. 'No Action' is clearly about someone regretting the failure of a relationship, yet it contains about half a dozen references to telephones. This is the first example of the album's obsession with various sorts of machinery.

'This Year's Girl' takes us from the personal concerns of the preceding song to the public issues of 'Welcome to the Working Week'. This song from *My Aim Is True* is partly about the exploitation of a female model, a theme Costello enlarges here. This year's girl of the title has achieved fame and become fashionable, her picture is everywhere. However, her success is only temporary; the title implies that she will soon be eclipsed and next year another girl will be in all the fashion magazines and on all the advertising hoardings. Even apart from the transience of her success she is dissatisfied: she is 'bored' being almost public property, so that everyone regards her as a saleable commodity. As time runs out and her dethronement gets nearer she begins to realise that she has been cheated, for what presumably looked like a glittering opportunity at the start of her year has proved to

29

be fool's gold. Only the failings of human memory make her predicament at all bearable: 'she's forgotten much more than she's lost'. If she were fully aware of the price she is paying, rather than just being vaguely discontented, she would not put up with it at all. She does not realise the full extent of her exploitation by men who have no interest in her except as a means to a fast buck. They use her and then cynically discard her, and, although the song does not specifically make this point, she is a symbol of all victims of sharp practice: like many of Costello's better songs it works on at least two levels, and the skill with which he handles these various layers proves him to be a writer of considerable sophistication.

As in 'No Action', the last verse is extended, but for a rather different purpose. Having already established that she is 'bored' Costello goes on to list some of the causes of tedium and the extended verse drags on monotonously, just as her life does. It's as if she spends her existence in some subterranean disco, mindlessly moving to the moronic metronomic beat. Deserts of vast eternity lie before her.

This brings us to another of the song's themes, which is, of course, time. Like 'Red Shoes', 'This Year's Girl' is an acrid complaint about the destructive nature of time, which consigns all material things to moths and rust. 'Time's running out' not just for the girl, but for everyone.

'The Beat' is a complex and in places confusing song about the doubts and anguish of adolescence and early manhood. It wastes no time in demolishing the myth of carefree youth by quoting from Cliff Richard's 'Summer Holiday', which temporarily produces a dream of jolly, clean-living guys 'n' girls, and then puncturing it by sinisterly mentioning 'vigilantes' who are apparently trying to catch the narrator. Add to this a crude sexual invitation and the vision becomes less like the Famous Five than Federico Fellini's *Satyricon*. Innocence receives another knock when sexual guilt is aroused when an unidentified man (perhaps a threatening authority figure) seems to enquire if the narrator masturbates, not a subject I can recall cropping up in Mr Richard's films. Even straightforward sex is apparently painful rather than enjoyable, though the morbid intensity of all this is undercut by the polysyllabic rhyme which produces a wryly humorous effect.

The song also portrays the social habits of teenagers. References to 'vigilantes' and 'walking down the street' hint at the ritual parades of mods, skinheads and so on, an interpretation supported by the often repeated phrase 'on the beat'. A beat can be a regular patrol (as in a policeman's beat), so one way of reading the song is to see it as a lament for the emptiness and monotony of youth culture, for a beat can also be unrelentingly unchanging, as in a disco beat. The song's inhabitants aimlessly strut around, trying to advertise their virility but instead revealing only their sadly suburban macho pretensions.

The last verse, mainly concerned with amplifying Costello's persona, culminates in the statement 'I don't wanna be your lover, I just wanna be your victim'. The apparent masochism here is perhaps really a way of keeping at a safe distance the frightening prospect of love, frightening because the narrator lacks the maturity to cope with the responsibility. Hence also the unconvincing nonchalance of the last unrepeated line, in which he brazenly pretends that there are plenty of other women waiting to hear from him, trying to make his lover think that he couldn't really care less about her. As in 'No Action' he tries to appear cool and collected but gives himself away with every line. Costello's psychologically incisive studies of outwardly cocksure but inwardly perplexed youth are some of the best things to be found in his early songs.

The bewilderment and torment of the narrator are excellently expressed by the song's complex structure – it can't easily be fitted into the normal pattern of verses alternating with choruses – and by the insistent organ riff (of two rising four-note phrases) that buzzes through it like a spiteful wasp around a donkey's ears.

Michael Gray, in *The Art of Bob Dylan*, traces the ancestry of 'Pump It Up' from Chuck Berry's 'Too Much Monkey Business' through Dylan's 'Subterranean Homesick Blues'. All three songs are basically lists of grievances sung to a virtually single-note tune. Costello's contribution to this tradition is a tremendously energetic and enjoyable attack on chic society (or at least people who like to think that they are members of chic society), and in particular on one of its female members. It is enlivened by a bludgeoning guitar riff that makes heavy metal sound subtle, and frantic Betje-manic rhyming. 'Pump It Up' is set in a 'pleasure centre', presumably some kind of nightclub. By giving the club this name Costello draws attention to its clients' thoughtless hedonism, and he also highlights their arrogant self-advertising, their malice and their empty-headedness. Their existence is weary,

31

stale and flat as a hedgehog unmindful of the Green Cross Code, and so they have to 'pump it up', inflate their egos and emotions, in a desperate attempt to make their lives seem meaningful. Such is the vigour of Costello's denunciation that his attitude is best described as disgusto.

In his biography of Costello Mick St Michael astutely points out that the harmonisation of 'Pump It Up' is deliberately limited. Usually tunes are supported by at least three chords, but this song has only two, (the dominant chord is missing), so the listener is left waiting for something that doesn't arrive and thus shares the feeling of lack of fulfilment.

'Little Triggers' has much in common with 'Alison', though neither the lyrics nor the music are quite as good as those of the earlier song. Nevertheless, it is a fine bitter-sweet almost-love song about a relationship that is dying through the woman's indifference. She is not unlike the woman in 'Miracle Man', given to making spiteful and sarcastic remarks, shooting out snide comments every time she opens her mouth. The narrator sees through her character and tries to persuade himself to be not so reliant on her, but as in 'No Action', he can't prevent himself being nostalgic and wishing that he could recapture the past. The song is touching because we sympathise with his predicament, which is echoed in the delicate little tune. For the first time Costello abandons the traditional rock rhythm of four beats in a bar in favour of six, creating a graceful minuet-like feeling that beautifully expresses his fragility. What's more, 'Little Triggers' fails to end on the tonic chord, the home key that the ear naturally expects a piece of music to finish with, leaving the listener with an appropriate sense of incompletion.

If you saw the title 'You Belong To Me' in a list of Top Twenty hits you would expect the song to be masculine assertion of conjugal and proprietary rights. In fact Costello once again confounds expectations by writing under this title what turns out to be a rather anarchic plea for sexual freedom, and perhaps by analogy social and political freedom too. The lusty bass riff with which the song begins soon banishes any gloomy introspection that might be left over from 'Little Triggers', and Costello then launches into his assault on 'you girls'. He is appalled by their lack of intitiative and timidity and rejects all they stand for. He doesn't want to conform to their conventional, restrictive standards, and certainly doesn't 'want anybody saying "You belong to me" '. In 'Blame It On Cain' from *My Aim Is True* he bewails his lack of freedom, and while 'You Belong To Me' does not go as far as saying that he has found freedom he certainly sounds determined to get it, which is a progression from the fatalism of the earlier song.

If some of the sneeringly violent lines in 'You Belong To Me' might be regarded as being in dubious taste, then the next song is pretty consistently stomach-churning. 'Hand In Hand' (another title whose romance is illusory) is, surely, one of Costello's nastiest songs. It was apparently inspired by bitchery and back-biting among some rock performers, though there is nothing in the song to specifically suggest this and it could equally well be the address of a man to his lover. The narrator is involved in some kind of internecine feud, and its chief motive is revenge. If the song is taken literally, then he has hired some 'bully boys' to do his brutal work for him; a slightly more charitable reading suggests that here his power fantasies are mingled with an unsavoury relish for violence. Brutality culminates in the rhetorical question, 'Don't you know I'm an animal?' As in 'I'm Not Angry' and 'No Action' the narrator attempts to deal with his chaotic emotions by denying that he has any feelings at all, as if to do so could excuse his barbarity.

Songs like 'Hand In Hand', in which the narrator's vindictive character is allowed free rein without any obvious self-doubt or distancing irony to make it clear that Costello is not speaking for himself, crop up occasionally on his albums – for example *Punch the Clock*'s 'TKO (Boxing Day)'. In the case of 'Hand In Hand' the pill is not even sugared by the unremarkable tune. Presumably Costello intends the listener to feel sickened by the narrator, but as the song contains almost nothing to signal this we are left wondering if this is really the case, and the suspicion that we are meant to side with the narrator enters our minds. If this suspicion were correct then 'Hand In Hand' would be not simply a song about a revolting person but a revolting song. Literature has always dealt with, and must deal with, bad characters as well as the good and the indifferent, but is there any value in such an apparently uncritical portrayal of gloating malignity, even if the original intention was satirical?

'(I Don't Want To Go To) Chelsea' is another song scorning fashionable society. Its chief attraction is the spasmodic bass riff and its dialogue with the guitar, which creates a sense of unease and even of foreboding. The lyrics too are episodic rather than all of a piece. The first verse introduces a lecherous man and a girl whom 'they call . . . Natasha' even though 'she looks like Elsie'. This is a witty way of indicating the egotism and fakery of Sloane Rangers and their like, (and a neat solution to the problem of finding a rhyme for 'Chelsea'). She is 'last year's model', and although the song is not precise about her present status (just conceivably she is a prostitute) it's clear that time has already run out for her and she's fallen from the heights of the billboards down to the streets if not the gutters.

The second verse is sinister though rather vague. References to 'new orders', 'warders' and 'men . . . in white coats' remind me of the fact that side two's last song, 'Night Rally', is about neo-Nazism. It is tempting to speculate that Costello is hinting that seedy exploitation hidden beneath a veneer of pseudo-high society might contain the seeds of fascism and the conditions in which they could germinate and sprout. After all, 'Oswald and his sister' from *My Aim Is True*'s 'Less Than Zero' are portrayed as possessing a decadent glamour. But we need not allow such (perhaps fanciful) interpretations to prevent us from enjoying the song simply as a lively lampoon.

'Lip Service' is a minor song, but it moves along briskly enough. It is in essence another assertion of independence, addressed to a girl and to the world at large. The narrator criticises her, and it, for 'going through the motions' instead of spending their lives doing anything worthwhile or fulfilling. So he feels that he owes them no allegiance; on the other hand, however, he does admit that she has some kind of hold over him, and admits by the end of the chorus that despite his assumption of disdain he is actually anxious to hear from her. Clearly, then, he really wants to be accepted, and once again his self-reliance has proved to be just a proud front.

The main theme of 'Living In Paradise' is familiar: despite the media's attempts to jolly everyone along by erecting a florid façade, real life is fatuous and empty. The chorus, heavy with sarcasm, claims that we are 'living in paradise', but the rest of the song makes it clear that life is not so much like the Garden of Eden as Welwyn Garden City on a wet Wednesday.

Many of Costello's weaker songs contain lines that don't seem to fit, and 'Living In Paradise' is a kind of orphanage for images, for Costello seems to have used it as a refuge for lines and ideas for which he couldn't find a place in other songs. Thus it lacks unity, but acquires an interest of its own as a checklist of some of his themes and obsessions: the jealousy of sexual rivals; the eroding effects of time; the injured innocent abroad; the brutality of the real world; and even voyeuristic masochism. These are all jumbled together to no obvious purpose. One wonders why his favourite recipes did not also find a place somewhere.

'Lipstick Vogue' is another song about the agonies of imperfect love, a theme writers have been using for centuries and which has enough mileage left in it to last several more millennia yet. But in order to maintain the audience's interest in this potentially hackneyed subject it is necessary to present it in varied forms. In this song Costello is not far from simply recycling his own earlier material, and despite the Attractions' heroic efforts to breathe some life into the somewhat prosaic music, it remains stillborn. There is a handful of striking (which is not necessarily the same thing as good) lines, though: 'Sometimes I think that love is just a tumour' could stand as an epigraph for his personal songs. 'I'm not broken' is an expression of resolve, and indeed, although listeners in 1978 might well have assumed from the less than brilliant second side of the album that Costello was already over the hill, later albums prove triumphantly that he's still capable of a trick or two.

It has to be admitted that the album's final song, 'Night Rally', is also not a complete succeess – the tune, especially of the chorus, is dull and the lyric goes beyond the nightmarish into paranoiac hysteria. But at least it abandons the overworked territory of too many of the other songs and attempts to confront an overtly political subject.

'Night Rally' deals with totalitarianism, and in particular the way in which it insidiously infiltrates society. 1978 was the period of Rock Against Racism, a movement intended to oppose all forms of fascism, not least the National Front, which seemed to be gaining strength at that time. The danger as Costello sees it is that we don't take Mister Oswald and Co. seriously enough to regard them as a real threat, considering them simply 'dumb' and 'funny', but because of this they'll exploit our complacency and soon have us all scampering like well trained dogs to the 'night rally'. Night has always been associated with evil, and also implies that everyone will be kept in the dark.

The middle, which like that of 'No Dancing' is skilfully highlighted by a sudden and dramatic change of key, in this case from E to G, pictures the participants at the rally 'singing with their hand on their heart' (perhaps especially implicating the USA since 'The Star Spangled Banner' is sung with hand on heart). This militaristic nationalism is seen as a scoundrelly step towards fascism, leading to 'singing in the showers'. This suggests both hearty post-rugger sing-songs and the Nazi gas chambers. If we surrender our individuality to the mindless fanaticism of the multitude then we are on the road leading to concentration camps. In this atmosphere of mass mania any expression of liberal doubt or political wetness is seen as tantamount to treason, and is met with aggressive contempt. And remember that 'Night Rally' was written before Mrs Thatcher's Conservative government, which is so intolerant of dissent, came to power.

Although the National Front had little chance of gaining any political power in 1978, and a decade later is even less effective than it was, the song is not simply a relic of a campaign fought and won long ago. Costello implies that even if obviously fascist organisations are defeated there are still some that use what amounts to a form of covert totalitarianism for their own ends. The focus of the fervour at Costello's imaginary rally is not the swastika but a 'corporation logo', the designer emblem of a (probably multinational) company. Instead of swearing allegiance to the Führer the communicants at the rally pledge their brand loyalty to the advertisement-created corporate image. Such is the pressure to consume that those who fail to take advantage of the spurious, cut-price, never-to-be-repeated offers feel 'ungrateful' for not supporting the economy by buying enough 'souvenirs'. Souvenirs are generally tawdry trinkets, so the choice of this particular word effectively reminds us that many of the goods adverts persuade us to buy from multinationals are not really the bargains they seem to be.

Costello compares multinational companies to totalitarian governments because they both attempt to control vast numbers of people. In order to do so they need labyrinthine bureaucracies, hence the reference at the end of the first verse to names being collected, which on one level suggests the lists of citizens from which companies get names and addresses for junk mail, but more sinisterly also suggests totalitarianism's obsession with cataloguing its subjects, perhaps as a preliminary to eliminating potential troublemakers. (Incidentally, this is the earliest example of

36

Costello's curious and quite frequent references to names being written down.) So 'Night Rally' cannot be dismissed as concerning just an ephemeral and largely forgotten period of British internal politics: its true subject is another ancient but perennially fascinating theme, the exercise and effects of power.

This Year's Model, then, elaborates on one of *My Aim Is True*'s major themes: the exploitation of the gullible many by the powerful few. As on the earlier album those in charge are seen as cynical and selfish manipulators, most clearly in 'This Year's Girl' and 'Night Rally'. What's more, everyone else, whichever rung of the social ladder they're clinging to, is determined to climb up it regardless of how many other people they'll have to tread on to do so. This is most apparent in the songs involving the night club crowd, with whom Costello had presumably had some contact since the success of the first album. *This Year's Model* offers a hellish vision of the foul rag-and-bone shop of the human heart.

This is just as true of the personal songs, some of which are astonishingly savage. (An album entitled *The Tender Touch of Elvis Costello* is about as likely as ones called *Abba's Anthems to Marxist-Leninism* or *Cliff Richard Sings the Sex Pistols' Songbook*.) Women are not seen as the prime movers quite so consistently as previously, but happiness is still something only to be looked back on, as in 'Little Triggers', or longed for, as in 'Lip Service'. The turbulence of the lyrics is exactly expressed in the overall sound of the album. I have the impression (which isn't literally true) that everything is taken at a frantic pace and maximum volume. The Attractions, in contrast to the easy-going musicians on *My Aim Is True*, provide a thunderous, unfettered and uncompromising accompaniment to Costello's cajoling vocals, at times sounding like a psychopathic accountant, with Nieve's keyboards especially prominent. The listener finds himself being thrown around in a maelstrom of sound.

Violent imagery is also prominent, but more interesting are the frequent references to various mechanisms, in particular telephones, cars, cameras and guns. This helps to build up a picture of a depersonalised world where there's no place for feelings, except anti-social ones such as greed and revenge. The album's mechanical imagery is generally used in unpleasant or negative contexts – even telephones become instruments of non-communication. Most interesting of all are the allusions to cameras, films and photographs. They remind us that the front sleeve shows

37

Costello with a camera pointing directly at the onlooker, as if he's about to capture us on negative as a preliminary to analysing our failings. This in turn stresses the album's emphasis on observing rather than actively participating: the sleeve of *My Aim Is True* shows Costello as the outsider, and the same is true here. His method is to watch like a photographer and comment, not to get involved. (This, though, is a simplification, because of course he does get and is involved, but all his involvements cause pain, so as in 'No Action', for example, he tries to distance himself.) The album is like a series of snapshots; he remains safely behind his Hasselblad, and *click*! he catches the plight of a model, *click*! he's got the anguish of adolescence, *click*! the agonies of unrequited love are stuck in his book. Thus bewildering reality is ordered and tamed. The camera can even be used as an offensive weapon, as in 'Living In Paradise' where the narrator gets his revenge on (presumably) his ex-girlfriend by watching a video of her making love with her new boyfriend.

The theme of the confusion between reality and artifice has already surfaced in 'Watching The Detectives', where the artificial film becomes more real than reality, and illusion has a significant role to play in *This Year's Model*. So, for example, in 'Pump It Up' everyone desperately pretends to have emotions that aren't really there, in 'This Year's Girl' the model is seduced by false promises, (and she is bored by synthesizers, creators of the unreal), and in 'Living In Paradise' it is suggested that we all live in an illusory Elysium that's actually more like Hades. We are constantly being deceived, so we can't even tell truth from falsehood with any certainty.

The blistering 'Radio Radio' revives *My Aim Is True*'s assault on the media. Costello is incensed by the blandness of pop music played on the radio, and is roused to an anything but bland riposte. The second verse is a kind of summation of Costello's early public songs: a few people are sufficiently vigilant to be aware of what's happening and are deeply disturbed by it, but the great majority are quite content to allow themselves to be manipulated in return for mindless pleasure. Those who run the radio (and by implication those in charge of other media) are out to 'anaesthetise' people's feelings, and, although this is not explicitly stated, we can assume that the purpose of this is to control the listeners by putting them into a relaxed, unthinking state of mind. With heads emptied of thoughts and feelings they'll obediently march off to the company's and party's rallies. The horror of this thought fires a simply tremendous song, one of the most exciting of Costello's rockers. His rage is such that the curious hissing noise in the chorus is probably the steam coming out of his ears.

'Stranger in the House', which was given away as a bonus single with early copies of the album, is a song about a failed relationship, and is Costello's first flirtation with country music. It's ingenious and, if you accept the rather maudlin melodrama of the genre, touching. The narrator portrays himself as very much a loser and outsider, but the recriminations of other songs are replaced by a gentle sadness.

'Big Tears' (the B-side of 'Pump It Up') is a macabre song about the meaninglessness of life and the inevitability of death. It begins with the extremely arresting image of everybody blithely going about their daily business while 'the sniper just takes his aim'. This horrifyingly brings home to us the fact that death can strike at any time. The chorus equally bluntly points out that remorse, the 'Big Tears' of the title, is futile in the face of mortality. The song's bleak lookout is similar to that of 'Waiting for the End of the World', and it's a chillingly effective *memento mori*.

'Tiny Steps' (the B-side of 'Radio Radio') is strange and gruesome. The lyrics are ambiguous, but the narrator appears to be relishing dominating and brutalising a woman, (referred to as 'baby', a rather patronising endearment; together with the constant emphasis on 'tiny' this leaves open the even more gruesome possibility that the song is about a real baby). If taken literally the references to 'lashes' and 'gashes' and to forcing her to kneel are revolting. Unless there's some other interpretation that I've missed this must rank as the most extreme example of disgust for women among Costello's songs.

One oddity from 1978 is the 'Dallas Version' of 'Less Than Zero', which appears on the semi-official album *Live At The El Mocambo* (released only in Canada). American audiences, unfamiliar with British politics, took 'Mister Oswald' to be Lee Harvey Oswald, assassin of President Kennedy, so Costello accordingly rewrote the lyrics. They focus on 'Jenny', presumably Oswald's wife, who is imagined making love with another man while watching the assassination on television. This continues Costello's love-hate affair with the USA: on one hand many of his strongest musical influences are American, but on the other, America is sometimes used in his songs as an example of all that's worst in the modern world. This is just one of the paradoxes of his music: violent yet vulnerable, cockily confident yet bewildered, scornful of love yet craving it, deeply pessimistic yet thinking it worthwhile to try to improve things, contemptuous of the underdog yet on his side. The more you look into his work, the more fascinating it becomes.

4

'Armed Forces'

The outer sleeve of 1978's *Armed Forces* is unique among Costello's albums in that it does not feature his picture. Instead the front shows a herd of elephants, the leading one glaring at the onlooker (as Costello does from the front of *This Year's Model*) and the back a medley of military scenes and abstract shapes and colours. Those responsible for marketing the album must have been confident that by now the public was sufficiently familiar with his appearance, and would buy the album on the strength of his reputation. They proved to be correct, for *Armed Forces* became his most commercially successful album so far, reaching number two in the British chart. Probably coincidentally, Costello's absence underlines the fact that his earlier volcanic persona has undergone fairly substantial modification. He is no longer quite so prone to exploding with accusations, and there's a lot less self-pity, (though he's still got a long way to go before he becomes as gentle or as sociable as an elephant).

This is immediately apparent in the opening song, 'Accidents Will Happen', which, although it deals with a familiar subject, the complexity and thorniness of human relationships, isn't concerned simply with furious finger-pointings. Instead, it presents a much cooler analysis, attributing the tendency of partnerships to self-destruct to two main causes: the pressures of living in a highly competitive society, and breakdowns in communication.

The verses mostly deal with the former cause. These are lyrically rather like a less frenzied version of 'Pump It Up', because although the location is not specified we sense the ruthless one-upmanship and backstabbing that take place amid the 'sweat and smoke'. This phrase, though extremely simple, effectively evokes a hellish atmosphere of exertion, fear and high pressure. Everyone feels that they have to keep up their sophisticated images and so are in a state of constant tension, unable to relax, and in these supercharged circumstances it's inevitable that eventually someone will crack, and 'accidents will happen'.

The chorus is tragically affecting. The rolling rhythm of the verses is abruptly halted by staccato chords, and the key is equally abruptly wrenched from D major to D minor, (the same modulation that gives the middle of 'No Dancing' its poignancy). This makes me wince with excruciatingly pleasurable pain whenever I hear it: the vocal of the verses ends on F sharp, but then immediately swoops up to a high F natural at the start of the chorus, the leap of a diminished octave creating just the right effect of agonised regret. Most of the C sharps are flattened to naturals too, so the ear hears the chorus as laced with blue notes. This is entirely appropriate to the melancholy words, which express the damage done to people's feelings in terms of road accidents. Drivers are under a lot of stress from other road-users, and this is one of the most important reasons for their making dangerous mistakes, so this is a good metaphor for the pressures of a competitive society.

The last line of the chorus is unique in Costello's work so far. On the first two albums his persona is quick to blame everyone and everything else, and especially the woman, for the inadequacies of relationships, without ever suggesting that part of the fault might be his. (A few songs, such as 'Sneaky Feelings' have vaguely hinted this, but only in passing.) But 'I know what I've done' is as specific an admission of guilt as you could hope for. For the first time he recognises that it is counter-productive not to acknowledge that it takes two to make an argument, and consequently accepts some of the blame himself. This self-realisation is rather moving, and helps to make 'Accidents Will Happen' one of Costello's best songs.

This would be true even if it consisted only of verses and chorus, but he's not content to leave it at that and slips in his masterstroke, the middle, which although only two lines long seals the song's success. The middle (also emphasised by a temporary key change, to B minor) is about the way people hurt each other without even realising they're doing so. Virtually all relationships must suffer at some time from failures to communicate, so we all know what he's singing about. Again this is something that can't simply be blamed on the other partner, it's everyone's fault, and the song brings home to us the heartbreaking inevitability of such pain. It's a sad song, but somehow strangely heartening too.

The two previous albums began with a personal song and a public song, and *Armed Forces* continues this pattern. 'Senior Service' is about the ruthlessness of big business in putting down those who aren't sufficiently quick or callous to grab power for themselves. The chorus (which begins the song) is based on a witty contrast between four short chords and eight staccato notes rising in comically indignant fashion through an octave and a half, providing effective musical pictures of the complacent, self-satisfied superior (the managing director, perhaps) and his envious minion.

The narrator's envy, presumably fired by the sheer injustice of his position and that of his boss, is given vehement expression in the verses. So vehement, in fact, that the narrator makes no secret of having violent fantasies of dismembering his boss, which if anything makes us feel less sympathetic to the underdog, but does show how ruthlessness breeds ruthlessness. The references to beheading remind us of the French Revolution, a similar example (if on a much larger scale) of the abuse of power and its results.

The short middle shows the authorities attempting to neutralise the narrator's hostility by appealing to his selfishness. In the process, though, they allow their cynical amorality to be revealed, like respectably dressed city gents glimpsed sporting leather bondage underwear. Although they're superficially civilised – it's quite easy to be so with plenty of money – beneath the veneer they're as barbaric as mobsters. Like the Mafia too they stick together, conspiring with one another to make sure that only the already powerful get given important jobs; their self-serving is indicated by the song's title.

Another connotation of the title is the navy, traditionally known as the senior service. This is the album's first reference to 'armed forces', which are the subject of the next song. 'Oliver's Army' is probably Costello's most celebrated song, the gloriously singable tune and the sweeping lyrics justifying this. Its main subject is military imperialism, but the skill with which this is shown to be part of economic imperialism further accounts for the song's status. Its narrator, although his position is never precisely stated in order to increase the song's universality, is presumably a British soldier serving in Northern Ireland. He's part of 'Oliver's Army' because one of the worst incidents in the history of Britain's suppression of Ireland was Oliver Cromwell's invasion and pillage of 1649, and the subsequent Acts of Settlement and Satisfaction which in effect made Ireland a province of England. The present troubles stem partly from Cromwell's actions, which are an example of imperialism, which in this context means the brutal exploitation of a weak country by a powerful country. The subjugation of the weak by the powerful is of course the subject not only of the previous song, but of several songs on the first two albums, so 'Oliver's Army' is pursuing one of Costello's perennial themes on a larger, macrocosmic scale.

Britain's mistreatment of Ireland over the centuries is not the only example of imperialism, however; the song alludes to several other places in the world where conflict arises from one group of people using military or economic might to take what is not rightfully theirs; Berlin, Hong Kong, England (because parts of it are bought by oil-rich Arabian states), the Middle East, the Chinese borders and South Africa. No attempt is made to elaborate on any of these – to do so would be nearly impossible in a short rock song. No doubt the issues raised by these allusions are very complex, with no straightforward answers, and could keep several *Any Questions* teams going for days on end, but it's not the purpose of the song to be glibly condemnatory. Instead, rather than just taking sides, it attempts to point out how widespread imperialism is, and how ugly are its results.

Imperialism would be powerless itself if it didn't have its lackeys, its soldiers, bureaucrats and so on, to do its dirty work, and the song's sub-theme examines the small-scale economic imperialism that traps people into becoming pawns in its game. In a time of mass unemployment joining the army must seem a reasonable proposition to some people, especially as the army tends to market itself as a provider of respectable, even glamorous jobs. Its advertising used to proclaim 'Join the Professionals' (maybe it still does), which implies that being a soldier is like a slightly more exciting version of being a solicitor or teacher. In fact, of course, soldiers are trained and paid to, in the last resort, kill people. The song points out that once someone has been seduced by the lure of what looks like a decent career they find themselves being exploited by having to shoot people they have no quarrel with. So the ironic situation arises in which the people shooting at each other ought to be on the same side of the metaphoric barricade, united against the real enemy.

44

This description of the song probably makes it sound like a naively simple analysis, but this is because I'm trying to spell out what Costello is content to leave only implicit. Like most of his songs it's got a narrator with whom we can identify and sympathise, which means that when listening to it we hear it first of all as the narrator's lament for his iniquitous position. There's the poor sucker, thrown into something he probably doesn't fully understand and certainly doesn't approve of, but with no way of escape. It's only once his wordless cries of distress have died away at the end that we begin to consider why he's in this position, and then we realise how skilfully Costello has blended together the theme of the soldier's predicament with the theme of military imperialism. 'Oliver's Army' is a great song because it finds a perfect metaphor in the private fears of the soldier for what's happening all over the world.

'Big Boys' is probably side one's least essential song. It's addressed to a man who's in the thrall of a woman, who is another incarnation of the woman in 'Miracle Man', though not portrayed as viciously as elsewhere. The song's main interest is its attitude to the man. The narrator is torn between sympathy and contempt: on one hand he knows what it's like to pay court to an indifferent woman, (which is described in familiarly violent and unpleasant terms), but on the other he seems to despise the man for being so foolish. According to the narrator he is desperate to become a 'big boy', a phrase which recalls a child's view of adolescents, and so implicitly accuses him of immaturity. Seen in this light, 'Big Boys' is similar to 'The Beat' because it's about growing up and trying to cope with a cruel adult world.

'Green Shirt' begins as a description of a female TV newsreader (legend has it that Angela Rippon inspired the song) who reduces colourful and complex world events to simplistic banalities. So from the first verse it seems like a typical assault on the media, but changes direction in the chorus. Here it becomes a sardonic description of a siren-like woman preening herself, another familiar subject, but before the chorus is over the song goes scurrying off in a third direction, leaving the listener disorientated. Suddenly it turns into a sinister picture of betrayals and double-dealings, taking its imagery from spying, (including a reference to lists of names, as in 'Night Rally'). It's not entirely easy to reconcile these three threads, all pulling in different directions, but what Costello is probably trying to do is to establish a link

45

between personal behaviour and relationships on a much larger scale. If people treat their friends and acquaintances cruelly, as the woman in the chorus does, then presumably they'll behave with even less humanity to people they don't know. So the allusions to Gestapo-like interrogations and so on try to create a vision of a world where no one can trust anyone, where personal loyalty doesn't exist. This is very similar to Orwell's *Nineteen Eighty-Four*, in which children are taught to spy on their parents, for example. I'm not sure, though, that the song entirely succeeds in plaiting together the threads — the first verse, for example, while good in itself, is left sticking out untidily.

What lifts the song out of the ordinary is the music, a showcase for Nieve's almost orchestral keyboards and Costello's conspiratorial voice. One aspect of the composition deserves particular mention. The great majority of songs, once they've established a time signature, maintain the same rhythm all the way through, but 'Green Shirt' has a trick up its sleeve, so to speak. It's basically in 4/4, but in the second line of the chorus a beat mysteriously disappears so that one bar is in 3/4. (To see what I mean count from one to four, taking your speed from the four introductory chords, all through the song, and you'll find that by the end of the chorus you're out of sync. To keep up with the rhythm you have to once count up to three instead of four in the chorus.) This device ensures that there's something subtly 'wrong' with the song, making the listener feel uncomfortable, as if something's going on behind your back but you're not quite sure what it is. This feeling of uncertainty of course echoes the song's theme of suspicion and paranoia.

Why *green* shirt? Green is the colour of envy, but the woman wearing it is not envious, (purple, the colour of pride, would be more appropriate), though I suppose someone might be envious of her. Symbolically green has many connotations, among them life, because plants are green, and death, because corpses turn green. This is probably stretching symbolism to absurd lengths, but this association with life and death does fit in nicely with Costello's songs' image of women as near-goddesses, to be worshipped for the gifts they can bestow, but feared for the punishments they can mete out. I don't think anyone should tell Angela Rippon that she's regarded as a modern Isis — it might go to her head. Still, all this might be nonsense. The trouble with symbolics is that it's sometimes not much sym and a lot of bolics.

46

'Party Girl' is in some ways *Armed Forces*' equivalent of 'Alison' and 'Little Triggers', in that it's an almost-love song. The first verse is a dissection of the emptiness of fashionable society, harking back to *This Year's Model*, but in the chorus and second verse the narrator pleads with the 'party girl' not to dismiss him, even though he's aware of her dangerously hypnotic powers over him. He's like someone stuffing himself with chocolates: he knows that later on he's going to feel bad, but all the same the temptation is just irresistible.

The song also relates to 'Red Shoes' and 'This Year's Girl', because it concerns time. He's willing to go to any lengths to please her, but it's not in his power to stop time for her. This reminds us that any time we waste has been lost irretrievably — the hours she's frittered away teasing and flirting at parties are gone and can never be regained. The beautiful coda, (reminiscent of that of the Beatles' 'You Never Give Me Your Money'), one of the album's grandest moments, is like an elegy for wasted time.

'Goon Squad' develops the theme of 'Oliver's Army'; underhand recruitment. It takes the form of messages from a young army recruit to his parents, telling of his experiences. In the first verse he is fairly wide-eyed about the opportunities that seem to be opening up before him, (promises of promotion, for example), though the cynical listener will recognise these as subterfuges. In the first album's 'Pay It Back', for example, the authorities persuade the narrator to be a dutiful citizen by promising success and plenty if he toes the line: they never arrive. It's not hard to guess that the same is going to happen here, especially as the song becomes increasingly disenchanted as it goes on. By the last verse the recruit has had his humanity surgically removed, and he becomes a fully fledged member of the 'goon squad'. This description makes them sound bestial and moronic, like neanderthal Nazis. It reminds me of the frightening belligerent stupidity that you sometimes see in squaddies' faces. 'Goon Squad' gives the impression that we need defending from them, not by them.

It's probably apparent by now that on *Armed Forces* Costello is writing about the army as a metaphor. The implicit idea is that the military is like life, (and indeed vice versa), and while this is not stressed in 'Goon Squad' there are a few little hints. The lyrics are deliberately vague, so you can never be absolutely sure that they're about the army. They could almost equally well be about the police, or even big business. So the song can be seen as not just a tirade against the moral numbness of the army, but against that of all big institutions. They're seen as corrupters of innocence, as in the chorus where the recruiting officers (or personnel managers) are described as if they're dirty old men abducting little boys. The other ranks are the officers' source of anything but innocent merriment.

At first hearing 'Busy Bodies' is lyrically much the same as 'Big Boys', though enlivened by a snappy pop tune and arrangement. It's addressed to a man, with whom the narrator is losing sympathy, who is being frustrated by a woman, the latest version of our icy Isis figure. More interestingly, however, it's related to songs such as 'Pump It Up' because it's about the purposelessness of modern life. Everyone's 'busy' because they spend their time in a frenzy of activity (perhaps in an attempt to prevent the meaninglessness of their existences catching up with them), but all this activity shows no really satisfying results. They scuttle around like ants acquiring a second car, a third bathroom, but never reach the point where they can sit back and be satisfied with what they've got. They want more of everything, except ulcers.

They are busy *bodies*, not busy minds – and they're busiest of all sleeping with each other. This is alluded to in typically loaded terms, making the couplings sound sordid and incestuous. There's an especially clever subtlety in these allusions, because Costello takes his vocabulary from the world of finance – 'merger', 'partner', 'company' and so on. What's happening here is the reverse of the subtext of 'Goon Squad', which uses a large public subject as an image of a small private one. 'Busy Bodies' implies that these messy sexual encounters, with all their unfaithfulness and amorality, are like the corrupt cut-throat world of commerce. Ronald screws Nancy: Ronald's Rubber Goods plc screws Nancy's Naughty Nighties Inc.

'Sunday's Best' was written for Ian Dury, but as far as I know he never recorded it, which is a pity because it would suit his endearingly flat, pithy vocal style. It's about the popular Sunday newspapers, and the prejudices and hypocrisies they feed on and exacerbate. The English are portrayed as reactionary and racist, eager to deal with all troublesome foreign affairs with violence. They cling pathetically to the illusion that Britain is still a world power and that the mere appearance off a foreign shore of a gunboat flying the white ensign is enough to quell the restless

48

natives. These illusions of grandeur are sharply contrasted with the reality: people's lives are trivial and monotonous. In the chorus, for example, they are almost sad figures, ridiculous in their underwear. How their ancestors came to rule half the globe, God alone knows.

The Sunday papers are implicitly accused of dressing up their titillating pseudo-stories as important news that the readers must know. We're all familiar with the sort of thing – gay vicars and randy pop stars, all presented as pruriently as possible but with the pretence that such things are shocking and need to be exposed for the sake of public morality. Incidentally, the social level of the inhabitants of 'Sunday's Best' seems to me different from that of those of most other songs. Costello usually confines his cutting comments to the 'smart' set, but since the sort of newspapers referred to are read predominantly by the working class, this song is apparently about 'ordinary' people.

Armed Forces uses a variety of musical styles, from the Abba-ish pop of 'Oliver's Army', to the near heavy metal of 'Goon Squad' and the distorted music hall of 'Sunday's Best'. 'Moods For Moderns' is the closest thing there is to Costello turning funky, (which would be only slightly less improbable, you might think, than Norman Tebbit turning punk). It's based on a great jazzy chord, E9, but is lyrically cryptic and not very substantial. It's basically about the pain caused by the ending of a relationship, though there are some sinister undertones. The title is puzzling – what *are* moods for moderns? The phrase sounds like a preten-tious advertising slogan, trying to make some tacky goods sound up-to-the-minute and smart. (The album's inner sleeve features a parody of a paint manufacturer's colour chart, complete with ludicrous names.) Presumably Costello is employing it ironically – the real modern moods are not falsely sunny, but include such feelings as disillusionment, alienation and fear.

The last two songs attempt to draw together the personal and public themes of the album. 'Chemistry Class' is essentially a put-down of a woman, to whom the narrator is nevertheless attracted. But onto this personal theme is grafted, none too successfully in my opinion, the public issue of the world's cruelty and in particular that of the Nazis. The last line of the chorus mentioning 'the final solution', intended to bring to mind Hitler's policy of exterminating the Jews, just sounds like a clumsy attempt to make the song seem portentous. However, although 'Chemistry Class' is probably the album's least successful song, it does show Costello clearly (too clearly, in fact – there's no subtlety) trying to suggest that the prejudices, insecurities, inhumanities and so on that caused the Holocaust are dormant in England in 1979, and perhaps therefore in most human societies.

This idea is pursued in 'Two Little Hitlers'. The verses sketch contemporary society, as seen through the narrator's eyes. Once again he is entangled with a cynically calculating woman, for whom he is apparently competing with another man, and the inhabitants of 'toilet town' are seen as stupid, obsequious, greedy and soulless. This is all very familiarly Costellian, but the chorus and middle add a new dimension. To call someone a 'little Hitler' suggests that they are letting whatever tiny bits of power they have go to their heads, so the chorus firstly implies that the narrator and his rival will fight over the girl. However, seeing this song in the context of the album we realise that the implications are much wider – the 'little Hitlers' could be, though little in their small-mindedness, frighteningly big in other respects. Hitler was the leader of a political party, so our 'two little Hitlers' could be, for example, the leaders of Labour and the Conservatives; he was a national leader, so they could be, for example, the presidents of the USA and USSR. This last possibility is enlarged in the middle, where 'the world goes off' at the flick of a switch, which evidently triggers a nuclear war. This is the most extreme example of the possible results of rivalry between two self-important idiots, so megalomaniac and childishly stubborn as to be willing to go to any lengths to get their own way. The vision of their pouting faces and shrill voices as they squabble over who's going to play with the world is chillingly comic.

The album ends in deep pessimism as one of the little Hitlers vows that he'll return, suggesting not only that fascism is not dead, but also that this sort of jackboot behaviour is likely to erupt whenever two people, or groups of people, come into conflict. The men bickering over the woman behave like scaled down storm-troopers; we all have within us the potential to behave like this in the right, or rather the wrong, circumstances.

To make a rather sweeping generalisation, the first two albums are parochial, while *Armed Forces* is global. *My Aim Is True* and *This Year's Model* both concentrate on issues of immediate concern to the narrators – there's nothing at all wrong with this, indeed it's this that gives the best songs their overwhelming intensity. *Armed Forces*, on the other hand, attempts to broaden these horizons and deal with much bigger issues. To this end, as we've seen, Costello tries to unite the personal and public songs. The album's working title was *Emotional Fascism*, which survives as a kind of sub-title on the inner sleeve, and which clearly reveals this intention, implying as it does that personal relationships are governed by the same forces that dictate mass relationships. This idea is not especially new, in fact Costello has already used it himself in songs such as 'Pay It Back', but he hasn't used it before (or since) with such consistency.

The public-political songs are at the core of the album. 'Senior Service', 'Oliver's Army', 'Goon Squad' and 'Sunday's Best' all involve military power, a subject not previously encountered, except perhaps in 'Night Rally'. Earlier songs are about economic power and show how institutions control individuals, but these songs additionally show country controlling country. So 'Oliver's Army' is about Britain's use of military might to rule Northern Ireland, and 'Sunday's Best' alludes to the British Empire. 'Goon Squad' exposes the sub-human mentality of the army, and 'Two Little Hitlers' reminds us that the very existence of the world is threatened by military power. The army provides the album's central image: whereas the first two albums propose that the world is run by those sharp enough to manipulate the unwary and gullible, *Armed Forces*, as its title suggests, demonstrates that sheer brute force has a large part to play too. The big and the tough can get what they want (presumably this is the point of the front sleeve painting – elephants are the biggest and strongest animals in the jungle, though it's a bit unjust using them as a symbol of ruthless force as they're sociable and unaggressive creatures, not in the same league as mankind when it comes to bestiality). This point is driven home by frequent references to violence, and especially to dismemberment (in 'Senior Service', 'Sunday's Best' and 'Chemistry Class'), which bloodily impress us with the supposition that the army is no more than a gang of legalised mad axemen. In turn, since the army is an image of society at large, humanity has few qualms about resorting to violence.

Personal relationships are also seen as a kind of war of attrition, both sides using guerilla tactics in attempts to wear down the other's resistance. Predictably, not one happy relationship features on the album, though the narrators are less given to vindictive

51

denunciation in response to this. Women are still portrayed in places as fearsome viragos, but the general impression is that relationships fail because of people's innate brutality, regardless of their sex. Emotional fascism rules: lovers' hearts are pierced not by Cupid's arrows, but by swastikas.

Musically *Armed Forces* is Costello's most pop oriented album, though exploring a number of different styles within this format. As I've already mentioned, this ensured the album's commercial success, (and I might as well point out that I'm not one of those who regard 'commercial' as a synonym for bad). But there is a possible paradox here. Although I'm sure Costello doesn't want to be a purely didactic artist, with a 'message' to which everything else is secondary, the care he gives to his lyrics proves that he regards them as important. *Armed Forces* is dressed up in so many sing-along Elvis tunes and arrangements that there's a danger that the average listener will entirely overlook the lyrics and their meaning. In a perceptive article in the August 1984 issue of *Marxism Today* (one of the few intelligent pieces of writing about Costello), Simon Lockwood discusses the 'aural packaging' of 'Oliver's Army', claiming that most people who heard the single on the radio, or even bought it, were unaware of its anti-imperialism. This is, I think, a valid but not insurmountable point. It can equally well be argued that if the lyrics are important then the first step is to make them available to as many people as possible, in the not unreasonable expectation that a proportion of them will eventually wonder who Oliver is and go on from there. Maybe it's more subversive to use the standard Radio One song format to make radical political points than it is to make similar points from an openly rebellious, outsider's position. Think of Crass, for example, a very admirable group. Their discordant, decidedly non-pop songs get little radio play or commercial success and although their lyrics are always worth listening to, how many people actually do get a chance to listen to them? 'Oliver's Army' must have influenced more people's thinking than any of Crass's songs.

One aspect of the album's composition that deserves particular mention is the number of songs that have a middle as well as verses and chorus: no fewer than eight of them. This shows a distinct development from the previous albums. The number of songs having three almost-independent tunes not only adds greatly to the musical variety, disrupting the occasionally plodding monotony of verse-chorus-verse-chorus alternations, but also expands the range of the eight songs in question. In many of the songs the middle provides the emotional focus or adds another layer; this is especially true of 'Accidents Will Happen', 'Senior Service', 'Oliver's Army' and 'Two Little Hitlers'. As Costello approaches maturity as a songwriter middles become increasingly important and numerous, transforming otherwise mediocre songs into good ones, good into great.

Two good minor songs appeared on the B-side of 'Accidents Will Happen': 'Talking In The Dark' and 'Wednesday Week'. The first of these regrets the passing of a relationship, a familiar enough subject, but enlivened by several deft touches. Talking in the dark is itself a good image of intimacy, and at the beginning of the second verse there's a witty expression of self-disgust. The overall effect of the song is actually fairly benign; although looking back with nostalgic regret the narrator seems much less hurt and recriminatory than in many other songs.

'Wednesday Week' is something of a curiosity. It's addressed to a woman who, for all her protestations of love, will be indifferent to the narrator by 'Wednesday week'. Thus the themes of the fickle woman and the slow decay caused by time are combined. Its oddity lies in its musical structure: it begins as a fast rocker, using the same bass riff that crops up later on 'Luxembourg', but halfway through abruptly changes tempo (and key) and becomes medium paced. This shows Costello using B-sides to experiment with different structures, but presumably he wasn't satisfied since he hasn't used this form again since.

'Crawling to the USA', first heard in a forgotten film, *Americathon*, is something of a *jeu d'esprit*. It's all quite light-hearted, so too much significance shouldn't be read into it, but it's essentially an ironic commentary on the values symbolised by the US. The criticism is smiling rather than bitter, however. The song continues Costello's interest in America (*vide* 'Less Than Zero' and 'Night Rally'), an interest that reaches a peak in *Get Happy!!*, where transatlantic musical styles are uppermost.

5

'Get Happy!!'

One of my friends rushed out to buy *Get Happy!!* when it was first released in 1980, and protested indignantly when he was given an apparently shop-soiled sleeve. He was mollified when the assistant pointed out that he wasn't being fobbed off with sub-standard merchandise, because all the sleeves had the same intentional pre-worn design. We can imagine that he slunk out of the shop pretty sheepishly. (Had he slunk as far as anywhere other than the UK he would have been satisfied, because for some reason the pre-worn look was removed for the LP's release in other countries.)

The sleeve of *Get Happy!!* is as carefully conceived as those of most of the other albums. It is contrived so as to give the impression, when glanced at quickly, that it contains an original 1960s American soul album, perhaps from the Stax label, which has been played many times. This is indicated by the artificial wear and tear, and by the deliberately naff design (at least, I hope it's deliberate) of garish colours and geometrical shapes, such as was quite unaccountably considered groovy in the era of kipper ties and fishy substances. The purpose of these devices is to proclaim the album's musical allegiancies. It is very strongly influenced by such artists as Al Green and The Four Tops and other musicians from the Motown, Hi and Stax stables. The soul influences extend from the album's overall feel to near-quotations from particular songs. I'm not going to attempt to point out every reference, but the musical origins of *Get Happy!!* should nevertheless be recognised.

There's a puzzle surrounding the arrangement of the album's songs: it's unclear which side is side one and which is side two. The sleeve places 'I Can't Stand Up For Falling Down' first and

'High Fidelity' last, but the label on the record kicks off with 'Love For Tender' and concludes with 'Riot Act'. There are various other bits of conflicting evidence, too. This is either a mistake or an attempt to persuade the listener to treat both sides with equanimity. If the latter is the case then the attempt is hardly necessary, because both sides are stormingly good. However, Geoff Parkyn's authoritative discography places 'Love For Tender' first, so I'll go along with that.

The opening track (if indeed it is the opening track) gets the album off to a breathtaking start, leaving the listener exhilarated. 'Love For Tender' is a complaint addressed to a woman who rejects the narrator's advances, but the main impetus behind it is a virtuouso display of thematic punning. This stems from the simple pun found in the title: tender (affectionate) and tender (offer of money). Despite the song's subject, there are fifteen or so references to money and finance, implying perhaps that the woman is mercenary and materialistic. Certainly it suggests a world as lacking in sincerity and loyalty as that in 'Green Shirt', thus setting the tone for the whole album.

The almost gleeful lamentation of 'Love For Tender' is very different to the mood of 'Opportunity', one of Costello's more obscure songs. It's relatively quiet, even reflective, so the words are unusually clear in the sense that you can hear what he is singing, though not clear in the sense that it's immediately apparent what he's singing about. It's not easy to see the connection between the various stanzas, and furthermore the significance of some of the lines is mysterious. 'Opportunity' is the first of several cryptic songs on the album, and their obscurity can be irritating, though teasingly fascinating too. A tentative reading of the song could be as a dissident aside on the values and organisation of post-war Britain. The reference to a 'baby boom' in the first line certainly suggests a period of prosperity and optimism, such as this country experienced in the later fifties and the sixties, and the title and beginning of the chorus have connotations of full employment and never having it so good. So initially the song offers a sunny view of a land of success and plenty, where rags to riches stories are commonplace. This is, I suppose, the 'official' image of Britain, but of course Costello is presenting it only to undermine it.

The first worrying signs appear in the chorus, where a mysterious 'they' appear, never to be identified and thus sounding sinister and threatening. Even more sinister is the fact that they are apparently keeping the song's addressee (the listener?) under surveillance, the latest in a sequence of references to being watched and kept tabs on. This implies that far from being free to seize our opportunities and make our fortunes, in fact an eye is kept on us to make sure that we don't get too successful and start having ideas above our station. So the much vaunted 'pride of the nation', including equality of opportunity, is shown to be simply an advertising gimmick and actually a cause of national shame.

The narrator's search for a girl is presumably a parallel to the nation's search for economic success, for it seems to be equally unfulfilling. In the second verse sex and machinery are associated once again, implying that he gets no joy from her, as he gets no satisfaction from the job market. And in the last verse we are finally allowed a glimpse of the people who keep the opportunities for themselves, in the form of a comic and revolting vignette of fat businessmen sweating and grunting in some kind of health centre. The final lines of the last verse are, appropriately, an echo of the verses of 'Senior Service', which is also about someone who has failed to make it big resenting the way in which the successful try to make sure that success is kept in the family. The narrator of 'Opportunity' is powerless to do anything except hope for the deaths of the fat cats whose obscenely obese bulks block his path to prosperity, but he can at least snatch a few crumbs of comfort from their irredeemable ugliness.

The rancour of 'Opportunity' is to some extent continued in 'The Imposter', though it's frenetically fast rather than broodingly bitter. It's an attack on a man who's apparently won the affections of a woman in whom the narrator is also interested, and the pain and shame of rejection, as so often before, stokes the song's boilers. The rival is a loathsome Flash Harry, trying to appear macho but in reality being pathetically ineffective. This culminates in the last verse where he's wittily described as having 'double vision' rather than being 'double-jointed' – the woman wants him to perform acrobatic sexual feats but he can't hold his drink and gets brewer's droop instead. The narrator can hardly believe that she is taken in by him – to the narrator he is so transparently an 'imposter', a fraud, that it seems impossible that anyone should be fooled. This is of course one of Costello's recurring themes, sham façades that trick most people into accepting them as reality without looking behind them to see the depravity they disguise.

If 'Opportunity' is obscure in places, then 'Secondary Modern' is as enigmatic as a stone unearthed by archaeologists with an inscription in some unknown and untranslatable language. Yet rather than being simply annoying, the oracular nature of the song somehow succeeds in making it compelling. Most of the individual parts of the song are clear enough, it's just that they don't fit together in any obvious way. A secondary modern, for example, was a school in pre-comprehensive days for those who didn't make it to grammar school. Perhaps the phrase 'secondary modern' appealed to Costello because of its undertones of being of secondary importance in the modern world, which is the fate of most of the inhabitants of his songs.

The middle and last verse are addressed to a woman, and the narrator is pleading with her to accept him as a partner. He is apparently so desperate that he's willing to allow her to propose any terms, even though he suspects that she's going to use him and discard him like a condom. Consequently, the whole song is strangely sad and subdued; this is most apparent at the end of the last verse where Costello's voice scrambles up to a pained and poignant falsetto: a touching moment.

'King Horse' is, like 'The Imposter', a put-down of a man and a woman, and uses financial imagery, like 'Love For Tender'. It pictures them sitting together in some kind of sleazy nightclub, she tartily dressed and he 'sniggering', perhaps at the club's strip-show or at some smutty joke. The reference to 'showtime' might mean that the club provides entertainment, but also suggests that the couple are putting on an act, presenting a false front to the world and each other. There's plenty of dextrous punning; for example, all she will get from him are 'loose exchanges', offhand and insincere remarks, instead of the genuine affection she presumably wants. The echo of 'loose change', a random assortment of coins of no great value, emphasises his emotional meanness.

The chorus, though brief, is one of Costello's finest. The narrator has now seen through the smart pretensions of the couple (and of other similar people) and realises that they're 'king horse', at first a puzzling phrase that needs some explanation. The symbolism associated with kings and with horses is multifarious, but for our present purpose it's enough to know that both concepts can stand for unbridled power, especially the power of the self. Thus to call someone 'king horse' is in effect to accuse them of being driven by ruthless selfishness, of trampling over other people to reach their desires. Hence the 'brute force' mentioned in the chorus, though this is softened a little by 'tenderness'. Some part of such people, perhaps, recognises that this way of life is unsatisfactory and feels the need for less aggression and more gentleness. However, neither in the song nor on the album is there any but the most fleeting sign that people can live together in anything resembling harmony.

Like many of Costello's best songs, 'King Horse' has a magnificent middle. While the rest of the song is content to be vehemently accusatory, here a note of sorrow is allowed to creep in. The couple are 'fond of the fabric' (eager for material wealth?) and of 'fabrication' (addicted to a false way of life), a state of affairs which is both laughably absurd and intensely sad. And human emotions are never simple: their complexity makes them all the more painful, a point superbly emphasised by the agonised but ecstatic melisma on the word 'complications'. It's as if Costello is recognising the sombre fact that all our lives are equally prone to tragic complications.

In the last verse the narrator assumes an active role (rather than being simply the passive observer of the chorus). Because of the abrupt grammatical change of person it's hard to follow, but it appears that he is addressing a woman (perhaps or perhaps not the same woman as in the rest of the song), saying that if they ever end their relationship he doesn't want to hear again the song that she has perhaps asked the club's disc jockey to play. To begin with this sounds as if this is because the song would painfully recall memories of their happy romance. In fact it transpires that he was familiar with the song before their relationship began, and so that's the reason he doesn't want to hear it again – it would remind him of his carefree innocence before she blighted his life. This apparently deliberately callous remark changes the listener's perception of the whole song, and indeed the whole album. Previously we've been inclined to accept that the narrators are in the right and thus that their points of view are unbiased and correct, but now we realise that they are little better than the people they've been attacking. By suddenly involving his first person narrators in the action like this, Costello must be inviting us not to accept blindly the narrators' moral superiority. Almost all the *Get Happy!!* songs have narrators, and 'King Horse' reminds us that they too have human failings. In effect this is an admission of guilt, like that in 'Accidents Will Happen', that both makes the narrators seem more vulnerable and so more sympathetic, (oddly so considering the gratuitous cruelty of the last verse), and their victims seem less contemptible since we know now that what we hear of them is only one person's opinion. This is very welcome, otherwise some of the songs seem very unpleasant indeed.

'Possession', a bitter song about a failed relationship, begins with an ironic near-quotation from the Beatles' 'From Me To You'. But while the original song sends love, Costello implies that money is what should be sent here – a purely platonic relationship. This is emphasised in the chorus, consisting only of the obsessively repeated title, which suggests the claustrophobia of an unhappy marriage in which one of the partners treats the other like an object to be bought and owned. This also contributes to the album's recurring theme of finance and business. 'Possession' hasn't got anything startlingly new to say, but it says what it says efficiently and with, after some of the earlier cryptograms, refreshing directness.

The opening verse of 'Man Called Uncle' is rather laboured, but otherwise the song shows Costello on top form. It expresses distaste for a woman and the older men, whom she coyly addresses as 'uncle', who pick her up. They're not described in much detail but are evidently like the businessmen in 'Opportunity', descending into seedy bars after work hoping to revive their flagging egos and libidos by chatting up available women. In the second verse the narrator attempts to deny all interest in the woman, but as several times before the middle is the emotional heart of the song. Here she is pictured apparently getting up after a night spent with the narrator, and, rather than describing her contemptuously, he obviously has sympathy for her and the rootless, unsatisfactory life she leads. He even goes so far as to admit that he is 'so affected' by her, a feeling beautifully echoed in the music where the F sharp of the key signature is flattened to F natural, the blue note cutting the listener's emotions like a surgeon's scalpel. This sudden turn around in his attitude is completed in the last verse where he hints that even though she's got her faults, she means more to him than do the other women he meets. So in the end 'Man Called Uncle' falls into a familiar pattern: he is outwardly indifferent to her, but this is just a mask to preserve his dignity which slips to reveal his real face, which is that of a man who craves love.

'Clown Time Is Over' is one of the hardest of all Costello's songs to understand, yet despite its difficulty (or because of it?) it's one of my favourites, especially in the slower version found on *Ten Bloody Marys and Ten How's Your Fathers*, where the churchy organ provides an appropriately hymn-like atmosphere. Its vagueness (which is presumably deliberate, since in most of his other songs Costello demonstrates his ability to write clearly when he wants to) seems to hint at all kinds of possibilities, so that it resounds in the listeners' ears and mind more resonantly than many of the other more straightforward songs.

What is clear about it is that it is some kind of lament. The title suggests that the time for light-heartedness has finished, and the dominant impression given by the song is that of regret, (again especially in the slower version). This feeling is musically reinforced by the mournfully flattened notes in the chorus and the instrumental section that follows it. The lyrics contain several sinister references that could have connotations of the brutal criminal underworld – 'blackmail', 'ransom', 'somebody's watching', 'a voice in the shadows' and so on – which create a subliminal vision of a threatening evil encroaching on our lives. Love, along with other ordinary human constructive preoccupations, has to be submerged in a cut-throat world – a prophetic suggestion at the dawn of the hard-headed eighties.

'New Amsterdam' musically stands apart from the other songs on the album, because it owes nothing to the rhythm'n'bluesy soul from which the others originate. Instead it is predominantly acoustic, in 3/4 time; it has something of the feel of a folk song, (and in fact the tune of the verse and chorus is purely in the old mixolydian mode, in which the seventh note of the modern major scale is flattened), and provides a welcome rest from the unrelenting aural assault of most of the other songs.

Although *Get Happy!!* was recorded in Holland, and despite several Dutch references, 'New Amsterdam' does not seem to be primarily about the Netherlands. Until 1664 New York was known as New Amsterdam, so the song actually returns to one of Costello's favourite subjects, America, or at least the way of life and system of values symbolised by America. (The song's promotional video emphasises this point by ending with a shot of the Statue of Liberty.) The first two verses are addressed to a typically Costellian woman (though, like the Statue of Liberty, she could be a personification of America), whom the narrator is simultaneously attracted to and rather scornful of. New Amsterdam is 'much too much', suggesting that it (and she) is initially irresistible, but (like cream buns) ultimately overwhelmingly emetic: Costello's ambivalent feelings towards America are perhaps represented here.

The middle and last verse combine nostalgia for a past spent in 'Liverpool and Rotherhithe' (apparently an autobiographical reference) with a present in which, despite his settled and satisfied appearance, he feels 'like an exile'. Although 'New Amsterdam' at first seems relatively sardonic and detached, in the end it turns out to be one of the most heartfelt cries of an outsider since *My Aim Is True*.

'New Amsterdam' is a good song, but not one of the album's most immediately appealing or rousing, so is for me an odd choice of single. The same applies to 'High Fidelity', which brings side one to a close. It's addressed to an ex-partner who now has a new lover, and uses thematic punning drawn from radios and record players. Costello plays on the double meaning of 'fidelity' (good quality sound reproduction and faithfulness in relationships), which adds poignancy to the plea in the chorus, 'can you hear me?', where the narrator begs the woman to listen to him. Indeed, throughout the song he regrets that communications have broken down between them and allowed the other man to usurp his place. Again he feels rejected and excluded; the choky vocals make him sound as if he's at the end of his tether.

Neither of the songs did terribly well as singles, but side two's opener, a cover of Sam and Dave's 'I Can't Stand Up For Falling Down' from 1967, became Costello's second most successful single (after 'Oliver's Army'), reaching number four in the UK chart. He had from the first featured other composers' songs in his live act, and a few had even appeared as B-sides, but this was the first time a non-original popped up on one of his albums. It adds some authentic sixties atmosphere to the album, and it's not difficult to see why he chose this particular song – its tale of a painful love affair suits his familiar injured innocent persona as a wide-brimmed hat suits Humphrey Bogart.

'Black And White World' is a miraculously good song, seamlessly moulding together three of Costello's principal themes: time, the media and the warfare between the sexes, all set to powerful and gripping music. The title alone is a wonderful phrase, evoking both the early days of cinema, when monochrome photography was more common than colour, and memories of childhood when life was so much simpler, issues more black and white, than in the bewildering complexity of adolescence and adulthood. Like 'New Amsterdam' this is a nostalgic song, looking back to former days of innocence. (This nostalgia seems sincere, yet Costello is careful to protect himself against charges of having a naively simplistic view of the past by incorporating some stale clichés into the song. For example, the past was a time when 'men were men': a laughably trite phrase. Thus he manages to keep a foot in both camps by simultaneously longing for lost time and poking fun at some of the results of doing so.)

In those days dealings with women were relatively trouble-free, perhaps because they were mostly confined to fantasising about models, as in The Who's delightful song 'Pictures of Lily'. Passing time complicates things, however, and nowadays not only is the narrator entangled in a recriminatory relationship, but also the model is 'framed and hung up'. This is a neat pun (or rather two neat puns), working, as good puns do, on two levels – because framed portrait photographs are more sophisticated than pictures cut from magazines and sellotaped to the wall, and because she has been betrayed and become neurotic. In this case last year's model has decayed into a nervous wreck. Nothing good lasts: we have but a short time, and that full of misery. 'Black and White World' is a threnody for the past, though far from dirge-like: it's vigorous and combative enough to make you think that Costello is in the mood to take on intransigent reality and win. Certainly the song makes life more endurable for one minute and fifty-four seconds.

I've already mentioned that the title brings films to mind, and the middle is more specific. Here Costello alludes to the way in which people sometimes use the productions of the media as substitutes for real life, a subject already touched on in 'Watching the Detectives' and elsewhere. Some people, on the run from reality, escape to the past, some to fiction. Which is the most comfortable destination? The song doesn't say. Incidentally, film is especially significant in a song about time, for it is a means of preserving against decay. Photos outlast the people, places, and events they record, and the same goes for songs. One of the strongest impulses behind all art, including Costello's music, is to catch the present like a fly in amber, so when it turns to past it hasn't altogether evaporated. The instinct to preserve is very strong: you should see all the junk I can't bear to throw away.

'Five Gears In Reverse', powered along by a terrific bass and guitar riff that winds through the song like the thread that binds a book together, is at first hearing another cryptic song. The key can, however, easily be found in the title and chorus. The phrase 'five gears in reverse' implies that rather than progressing we are actually finding new ways of going backwards, and the chorus is specifically about hopelessness and futility. So, although some ingenuity is required to make the verses conform to this pattern, the song is another one about the pointlessness of modern life.

Despite the many technological advances that the twentieth century has seen, the lives we lead are no happier or more fulfilled than those of our ancestors, indeed, as many previous songs have made plain, we spend much of our time racing around vainly trying to fill our sense of emptiness. The song's thematic puns drawn from cars emphasise the materialism of modern times, and suggest that we are speeding faster and faster not towards a scientific paradise, but towards self-destruction. As we drive more and more recklessly, not quite knowing where we're going but wanting to get there quickly, sooner or later there's going to be an apocalyptic multiple pile-up. Costello's screams of anguish at the end (though they can also be read as yells of exhilaration in response to the infectious swing generated by the Attractions) and his feverish guitar solo conclude the song with an overpowering sense of imminent disaster.

'B Movie' is addressed to a woman, somewhat heartlessly and even sneeringly putting her down. The narrator at first disclaims all serious interest in her, even nonchalantly mentioning that he is accustomed to hit her, one of several references on the album to violence against women. This is certainly sickening enough, though by the end of the last verse it's clear that this show of aggression is an attempt to disguise weakness, and that really he's not as immune to her as he'd have us believe. The narrator here is a clear example of the sort of person who tries to relieve his feelings of personal inadequacy by beating up his wife or girlfriend (though of course I don't mean to imply that there can be any justification for such acts). Furthermore, the references to America and 'Britannia', although only made in passing and not enlarged on, perhaps relate 'B Movie' to *Armed Forces* by suggesting that personal violence and chauvinism are similar to the treatment dealt out by powerful countries to weak ones.

'Motel Matches', though lacking the brutality of 'B Movie', is not dissimilar to it. Again the narrator is involved in an unsatisfactory affair, which is presumably taking place at present in a motel room. He listens to the conversations and televisions through the thin partition walls, and thinks of the seedy sexual encounters being enacted in the other rooms, giving a sense of all the other unsatisfactory lives being lived all round. His feelings towards her are ambivalent, on the one hand he is doing his best to behave as a lover should, but on the other he casually dismisses her with as much thought as he'd use to give someone a light from a book of motel matches. There's none of the triumphant nastiness of 'B Movie', however, and the tone of the song is sober and despondent as the relationship goes up in smoke.

Ambivalence is even more evident in 'Human Touch'. The verses make no bones about his disgust for his partner and the world in general, which reaches such an extent that he begins to drink heavily and knock her about. In the chorus and middle, however, he is equally emphatic about his need for 'the human touch', which, it seems, only she can supply. It's hard to reconcile these two attitudes: the narrator must be seriously disturbed, even on the verge of breakdown. The song's spasmodic ska rhythms, sounding like the mad dance of a malfunctioning robot, echo the disintegration and degeneration of his mind. That he recognises this is evident in the middle, where his agonised long-drawn-out cry of 'Oh' makes you bite your lip and draw in your breath in sympathy, as if you were hearing about some gruesome and painful mishap. It's hard to maintain this sympathy, though, for in the last verse he has knocked her to the ground and stands over her, gloating. Mabye the song should be retitled 'Inhuman Touch'.

Such a distressingly crude and sexist view of women (and this is an only slightly exaggerated version of that found in several other songs) invites some kind of riposte, and Costello forestalls the listener's protestations by providing one of his own. 'Beaten To The Punch' is a furious assault on a man and his juvenile macho attitudes. Costello mercilessly exposes his petulant selfishness, his arrogant dismissal of people older and less trendy than him, his bullying of and leering at women. He's a familiar type:

most of us are probably unfortunate enough to encounter people like him, with their loud voices and loud behaviour, several times a week. Throughout the song runs the refrain 'almost beaten to the punch', suggesting that simply by acting aggressively he just about manages to keep one step ahead of the opposition, but by the last verse he's had his comeuppance. Time has had its effect on him, as it does on all things, and now he finds that he's becoming one of the older men whom he previously made fun of, and in his turn he's being laughed at. Success with the girls can no longer be counted on, and the song ends with the suggestion that the only option now open to him is to entice one with an offer of marriage. This is hardly a firm foundation on which to build a relationship, and his story, or the story of other people like him, is continued in later songs such as 'Shot With His Own Gun'. 'Beaten To The Punch' is probably the song I like least of all the songs on the album – the music has energy but little else to recommend it – but it's a necessary corrective to some of the other ones.

'Temptation' is a curious song, again addressed to a man (though the middle and even some lines from the verses could well be addressed to a woman), and which possibly concerns the inescapable pressures of living in a competitive and bureaucratic society. The lyric contains several words and phrases that seem to suggest a lack of freedom, a state of being constricted and watched, for example 'mumbo jumbo' (possibly a reference to bureaucratic jargon), 'threat of arrest', 'authority' and 'shackled up to the rigmarole'. In this respect the song is not unlike 'Opportunity' and 'Clowntime Is Over', as well as earlier songs such as 'Green Shirt', which evoke worlds controlled by sinister undercover powers. Having said this, the man to whom the song is addressed is apparently itching to get his hands on a woman, and it's by no means clear how this relates to the main theme, nor how the middle relates to the rest of the song. The whole effect is confusing and disquieting.

'I Stand Accused', a cover of an old Merseybeats' song, is the album's second non-original. It thunders along, and could easily be mistaken for one of Costello's own compositions, albeit a relatively routine one, since it uses thematic punning (concerning trials) and burns with incandescent intensity.

A similar passion smoulders in 'Riot Act', the album's last (and longest) song. This looks back on a failed relationship with abject desolation, as well as a few sparks of bitterness. The pace at which it is taken is fairly slow, though the rhythm becomes much more insistent in the climactic choruses, and this sombre speed allows Costello to dwell with relish on every vocal nuance. Throughout the song his voice sounds as if it's just about to crack up, as if he's reached the end of his tether. (And, after all the rebuffs of the foregoing songs, it's hardly surprising.) It's a tremendous performance, squeezing the last drop of emotion from the lyrics. Although the narrator does allow himself some acrimonious digs in the middle, in general he seems to be beyond accusations and counter-accusations and is in a state of unconditional surrender, waving the white flag to a hostile world.

And so ends *Get Happy!!*, an exhausting twenty-song marathon, (although because of each song's compactness and conciseness the album lasts not much longer than three-quarters of an hour). The number of songs is the most obviously striking thing about it – who but Costello would dream of cramming so much into so short a time? Most other rock musicians would probably include fewer songs on a double album, and many rock double albums are simply single albums with a lot of padding. While it's inevitably true that some of the *Get Happy!!* songs are better than others, none of them is, so to speak, mere foam rubber: they're all the real thing. Eighteen original songs poured forth at once is evidence of amazing productivity; such an overwhelming quantity is quite hard to take in, so it's more than usually necessary to stand back to try to get an overview of the album.

It might be helpful to begin by trying to sort out the songs into our two categories, personal and public. As I've already made clear, this categorisation needs to be treated with caution, and this is especially true in the case of *Get Happy!!* because virtually all the songs are in the first person and are at least partly about the narrator's troubles, and thus can be classified as personal. It won't help very much if we put all the songs into the same category, so it's necessary to try to decide which songs go on to make some kind of general comments about the nature of the world. Again, it would be quite possible to reply 'All of them', but I think this is a reasonable division: in the public or political category, we have 'Opportunity', 'Clowntime Is Over', 'Five Gears In Reverse' and perhaps 'Temptation', while all the others are personal, (unless we're going to invent a third category for songs about time, in which case 'Black And White World' belongs there).

Even though it's true that some of the songs I've classified as 'personal' could almost equally well be called 'public', 'Love For Tender' for example (since it's as much about money as about love), this division reveals that the emphasis of the album is very much on private concerns. The previous album, *Armed Forces*, is roughly equally divided between the two categories, and further-more even the personal songs are intended to reinforce a political theory. Maybe Costello was propelled by the thought that the 1970s were rapidly concluding, and so if he were going to make a concept album at all he'd better do it quickly. There's no similar emphasis on *Get Happy!!*: no more than a fifth of the songs are public. And the personal songs give the impression of being just that: deeply, intimately personal, so that you feel like a kind of aural voyeur listening to them. I'm not especially interested in how, if at all, autobiographical Costello's songs are, but you've got to have the sensitivity of a cabinet minister not to recognise that *Get Happy!!* springs from a deep well of intense unhappiness.

Costello has, of course, always written songs about relation-ships that are unhappy or finished, or both, but this trait now becomes an enormous disfiguring facial birthmark. It can't be avoided: even when you try to pretend it's not there, you keep being drawn to it with macabre fascination. Relationships now don't just fall apart, but explode like evil shrapnel bombs, riddling anyone unlucky enough to be in range. Accusations are not merely made, but gallons of vitriol are jetted out, napalming the whole vicinity. *Get Happy!!* is a great album, but one to be treated with the utmost care. If anyone bought it expecting to hear the Harold Arlen and Ted Koehler song of the same name they were in for a shock.

In many of the songs, as I've already noted, the narrators sound almost out of control, as if they're rapidly going under. In such circumstances people behave savagely, forgetting civilised behav-iour as they desperately struggle to survive. This accounts for the album's high incidence of violence. Again this is nothing new, but what is relatively new is the extent to which violence is directed at individual women. The violence on the previous albums has been used mainly to heighten feelings of rage, horror and confusion, but here the emphasis is on what amounts to wife-beating. 'B Movie' and 'Human Touch' both contain passages in which the narrators use physical force against their partners, and although Costello scorns such behaviour in 'Beaten To The Punch'

I think it's worth asking how or if this subject can be justified at all. This question is especially pertinent as several subsequent songs contain similar passages, such as 'TKO (Boxing Day)' from *Punch The Clock*, and in the light of the alleged misogyny of many of Costello's songs.

The essential justification must be that it's true. Some men do hit women, and Costello is presumably concerned with giving a faithful picture of the world as he sees it. Many of his other songs are about equally unsavoury subjects, such as fascism, but I don't think anyone would object to them on the grounds that such themes should be suppressed. What's more, violence against women is a semi-taboo subject, too often brushed aside in awkward embarrassment and certainly rarely dwelt on in rock songs. Thousands of songs adopt aggressively macho attitudes to women (the Beatles' extremely nasty 'Run For Your Life' from *Rubber Soul*, for example), but generally with the assumption that women really like being treated in this way. Costello tries to demolish such nonsense by confronting us with the harsh reality. And taking this argument one stage further, as on *Armed Forces* the implication seems to be that wife-beating is not just something that other people do, but that we all have in us the potential for aggression. This is not to say that 'all men are potential rapists', (a pretty ludicrous statement), but does mean that when we're cornered it's human instinct to lash out, physically or otherwise. Violence against women is, I imagine, usually the result of a man feeling threatened, and *Get Happy!!* tries to describe the circumstances in which this happens and women get battered. It would be going too far to try to claim Costello as some kind of feminists' champion, but at least he is taking a step in the right direction by forcing us to be honest even though it hurts.

Unpleasantness towards women is not confined to violence. Several of the songs seem to take pleasure in telling women how little they mean to the narrators, and while this is again far from unexpected the overall impression left by the album is more viperish than that given by the previous ones. On the other hand, although there's nothing to match the twisted tenderness of 'Alison' or 'Little Triggers', a roughly equal number of songs make it clear that the narrators are literally desperate for love. This paradox is behind the album's at once exhilarating and frightening sense of being *in extremis*, of being at the limits of endurance. This sense is wonderfully conveyed by Costello's version of sixties soul: the Attractions play as if possessed, as if there are only a few short hours left and as much as possible has to be crammed in. (Indeed, Costello and the Attractions did disband briefly after the completion of the album - they must have felt utterly drained, as if they'd given everything and couldn't possibly find any more resources to fuel a continuation.) Although at the limits, the album never quite goes over the edge, partly because of Costello's innate feeling for form, (I mean artistic form, not good manners), which keeps the songs tight and prevents them being self-indulgent, and partly because of his awareness of the redemptive powers of love. When you're staring down into the abyss, I imagine, you suddenly realise what your ultimate priority is, and for most of us this is going to be love. 'Human Touch', for example, in places one of the most vicious songs, recognises in the middle that love is the one thing that can save the narrator from falling. Despite all the snide remarks, despite all the brutality, despite all the off-handedness, he needs love, and this is what, in the final analysis, makes *Get Happy!!* bearable to listen to.

The public songs can be dealt with more briefly. The first thing you notice about them, apart from how few there are, is their lack of specificity. The media, previously a principal target, hardly get a mention, and instead we find fairly generalised cynicisms about society. As on the first album, it is implied that we are ruthlessly manipulated by smug Mister Bigs, who won't hesitate to crush the first sign of rebellion. This lack of development is perhaps disappointing, but to criticise the album for not being very political is like criticising *King Lear* for not containing the recipe for bread pudding – true but utterly irrelevant.

Two stylistic devices are particularly noticeable. The first is the number of songs that use what I've chosen to call thematic punning – that is, the inclusion of several references to a theme that is not what the song is 'really about'. This is a device not unlike the 'conceits' of seventeenth-century poetry, and which wittily binds a song together, and can offer some striking analogies too. The songs in question, together with their themes, are: 'Love For Tender' and 'King Horse' (both money), 'High Fidelity' (radios), 'Black And White World' (films), 'Five Gears In Reverse' (cars), and 'Beaten To The Punch' (boxing), (as well as the non-original 'I Stand Accused' (trials)). The nonchalant skill with which Costello yokes these themes to their 'true' subjects is one piece of evidence to prove him a song-writer at the top of his form. The second stylistic device is the use of a middle as well as verse and chorus in the songs: eleven out of the eighteen originals employ it. As on *Armed Forces*, the middles often add another dimension to the songs, suddenly putting everything into a different perspective. 'New Amsterdam' is a good example, where the middle transforms the song from a relatively academic exercise in well-worn themes to a profoundly evocative lament. Although it's true that *Get Happy!!* isn't Costello's most tuneful album, the musical ideas come flooding out of him. This incredible fecundity (of words as well as music) is one of the things that ensures the album's greatness. In my opinion, with this album begins Costello's most fruitful period which produced the trilogy of magnificent albums which forms the essential part of his achievement: *Get Happy!!*, *Trust* and *Imperial Bedroom*. And if I had to choose just one, despite the fact that listening to it repeatedly would probably make me suicidal, it would be *Get Happy!!*

Not content with the eighteen original songs on the album, Costello released another six during 1980, (not including 'Clubland', which appeared as a single in December, and eventually formed part of *Trust*). This means that, on average, he was writing viable songs approximately once a fortnight — how many other first-class song-writers are capable of maintaining such a workaholic rate? Furthermore, most of these six additional songs are of high quality. It says a lot for Costello's confidence in his talent that he was content to release them in relatively obscure formats.

'Girls Talk' is probably best known in the version by Dave Edmunds, which had some success as a single. This version is vigorous and catchily enjoyable, quite different to Costello's own, which first appeared as the B-side of 'I Can't Stand Up For Falling Down'. Here the song is relatively low-key and introspective, a collection of jumbled thoughts and impressions as the narrator listens to the conversation of a group of women. In some ways it returns to the view of women implied by *My Aim Is True*: siren-like, alluring but dangerous. Consequently he is torn between listening to their talk and keeping at a safe distance from them, and indeed the phantasmagoric fragments of conversation that filter through to the listener are alarming enough.

'New Amsterdam' was released both as a single and as an EP, the latter containing three songs in addition to the title track. The first of these, 'Dr Luther's Assistant', is a real oddity. Who the eponymous character is I can't say — the only Luthers I can think of are Martin Luther, the sixteenth-century Protestant leader, and Martin Luther King, the American civil rights leader, neither of whom have any obvious connection with the song. It does, however, revive Costello's use of cinematic imagery, not much seen since *This Year's Model*, and in the last verse displays his interest in voyeurism. The only other helpful comment I can offer is that, according to the chorus, the assistant might be some kind of gremlin, a symbol of the imperfectibility of all human activity.

Fortunately, the other two songs are much clearer, and much better. 'Ghost Train' is about unemployment and its effects, the first time Costello broached this subject which must have been in the thoughts of many of his listeners. Its protagonists are Maureen and Stan, presumably representatives of the thousands, millions, of ordinary people who, despite their talents, can't find a job. Consequently their lives and relationship gradually decay, a process described by an accumulation of astutely chosen details. They are enticed to ride on the 'ghost train', an evocative image because fairground ghost trains go nowhere, and because anything ghostly is insubstantial, suggesting that the only kind of jobs they are likely to find are grossly exploitative ones. 'Ghost Train' is a good song, dealing with an important subject compassionately but without being patronising, and never descending to mere sloganeering. Incidentally, could it have had any influence on the Specials' similarly targeted 1981 song 'Ghost Town'?

If the words of 'Just A Memory' were read without realising that they were part of a song, they would appear cold and even callous. The narrator says in so many words that the ending of his affair means next to nothing to him, is 'just a memory'. A more careful reading reveals this is at best only a half-truth – it's hinted that he's sleepless and drinking heavily, for example – but nevertheless the words basically state that he couldn't care less. However, as we've seen before, Costello's songs sometimes mean the opposite to what they at first seem to say, and this is so in the case of 'Just A Memory'. Listening to the song, rather than just reading the lyric, we are left in no doubt that he does indeed care, very deeply. The recording (which features only voice and Nieve's piano and organ, creating an intimate four-in-the-morning atmosphere) positively bleeds regret and sorrow, especially in the chorus where the double-tracked vocals strain upwards towards an exquisitely wounded falsetto. In effect, then, the words attempt to rationalise in order to neutralise the pain, but the music strips

71

reason away and exposes the raw emotion. And when you think about it this is inevitable in a song with this title, for how can Costello dismiss anything as 'just a memory'? Dozens of his songs reveal how much memories of the past mean to him; he lingers over them like a butterfly collector relishing his specimens. 'Just A Memory' is one of his most nearly flawless almost-love songs.

In November 1980 a collection of all Costello's songs not otherwise available on an album appeared, entitled *Ten Bloody Marys and Ten How's Your Fathers* in the UK and *Taking Liberties* in the US; (there were some variations in their contents). Considering that most of the songs on it were originally released only in dribs and drabs, on B-sides and so on, the album stands up amazingly well. If I were to arrange his albums in rank order, I'd certainly place it above at least two 'proper' albums, and probably even higher. Its wide variety of styles and subject matter certainly makes it endlessly entertaining, and as a bonus it contains two previously unreleased songs.

The first of these, 'Clean Money', is one of only two instances of Costello setting what are substantially the words of an existing song to different music, (the other is 'Big Sister's Clothes'/'Big Sister'). The song is essentially a version of 'Love For Tender', not quite as rousing as *Get Happy!!*'s opener, but nevertheless further fascinating evidence of Costello's willingness to experiment with material. He obviously doesn't regard each song as perfect and therefore immutable, but as the working material for variations.

If there were to be a competition for a beautiful song on the most unlikely subject, then the second previously unreleased song would surely win. 'Hoover Factory' is an idiosyncratic but profoundly beautiful song, which is doubly strange as 'beautiful' is not even a word normally associated with Costello's music. The song begins prosaically enough with a deliberately flat account of the Hoover factory, a 1930s building in Perivale, in what used to be Middlesex. Costello's eye had obviously been taken by it, hardly surprising for it's a striking piece of architecture in a mostly featureless corner of London. You might expect him to use the factory as a symbol of domestic boredom or capitalist tyranny, but in fact the words and tune lift lyrically in the chorus, and the song turns into a meditation on the relative values of human life and art. The demolition of the factory would not materially affect our lives, but then neither would Costello's death. Which is more important, art (that is, the factory) or the life of an individual human being? This is a crucial question: is it right to spend millions of pounds on paintings when a large proportion of the world's population lives on or below the breadline? And on a more day-to-day scale, can we justify spending a few quid on, say, a record we don't really need instead of donating the money to Oxfam? All of us living in relative affluence have to face this question. 'Hoover Factory' raises it rather than answers it, and we ponder it as the lovely coda shoots off into remote harmonies, then drifts back to the home key.

It's only fair to add that not everyone shares Costello's high opinion of the building – Sir Nikolaus Pevsner in his definitive *The Buildings of England* calls it 'perhaps the most offensive of the modern atrocities along this road of typical bypass factories' – but it's a quirky example of its period and far better than the office blocks, monstrous monuments to megalomania and Mammon, that would probably be erected if it were to be demolished.

It's fitting that such a good song should surface in 1980, for this emphasises just how creatively fertile this year was for Costello. Other rock musicians must have laid down their guitars in despair at ever being able to compete with such a formidable output. 1980 was Costello's *annus mirabilis*, his year of wonders.

6

'Trust'

From the front of 1981's *Trust* Costello peers over the top of his red-tinted glasses, (though he's not someone we normally associate with rose-coloured spectacles – we expect him to look at the world with more jaundiced eyes). His eyes don't meet the spectator's, gazing instead somewhere to his top right. The sleeves of the first two albums show him glaring straight at us; the sleeve of *Trust* promises a less confrontational approach, a less head-on assault and a more sidelong glance. Despite Costello's frequent warnings not to trust appearances, this is just what *Trust* delivers: the trend begun by *Armed Forces* away from the angry young man and towards the cynic who recognises his own culpability continues, after being partially diverted by *Get Happy*!! The motif of eyes looking over the top of glasses is also made much of in the two promotional videos of songs from the album, 'Clubland' and 'New Lace Sleeves'. So Costello's earlier persona has by no means been altogether left behind, for this motif suggests watching from behind cover. From the first he's been an observer, even at times a virtual voyeur, keeping a close eye on the events before him. The sleeve of *My Aim Is True* brings back childhood memories of Brains from *Thunderbirds*; the fictional character evoked by that of *Trust* is the man with X-Ray Eyes. In which direction is his penetrating gaze sweeping now?

The sleeve of *Get Happy*!! refers back to the 1960s; *Trust* looks back even further into the past, to the forties and fifties. The photograph and credits on the back are presented in the form of a pastiche of a film poster. Costello and the Attractions look not unlike a band providing tasteful background music in a hotel cocktail bar in a B-movie that surfaces from deserved obscurity on Channel Four on a weekday afternoon. It's not hard to imagine the camera panning away from them, across the tables to the hero and heroine, locked in a turbulent emotional scene. And if we turn to the inner sleeve we find an even more ambitious recreation of the period: the group is transformed into a twenty-one-piece dance band, no doubt performing some smoochy number. This photograph must have taken a considerable amount of time and effort to set up: the evocation of a post-war dance hall is created with loving attention to detail, down to the music stands monogrammed 'EC'; (Nieve's electric piano and one or two haircuts are the only anachronisms). The picture inevitably and no doubt deliberately recalls the fact that Costello's father was a member of the Joe Loss Orchestra in the fifties. The trouble that has been taken with it indicates the picture's importance to Costello; it stresses the significance of the past and of nostalgia. Although this is not a major theme of *Trust* it's an integral part of his work and is rarely buried too deeply. The picture also complements his use of nightclubs as a source of recurring imagery, and perhaps reveals an ambition to emulate his father. If so, this ambition was more or less fulfilled in 1983 when he toured London dance halls with an eleven-piece band.

But it's the photograph on the other side of the inner sleeve that really sets the mood. Here Costello is pictured in dark surroundings, his face and hands brightly spotlit, dressed in trench coat and trilby hat. He's just lit a cigarette, and the smoke from the match curls interrogatively. He looks uncommonly like a character from a *film noir*, those murky movies, especially prominent in the forties, about gangsters and the almost equally corrupt police who try to catch them. To be more precise, he looks like a private detective from such a film, on the trail of a particularly unsavoury case. His impassive face suggests he knows more than he's telling: his remarks will be sardonically drawled out of the side of his mouth. This is, along with the photograph on the front of *My Aim Is True* and one or two others, one of the most characteristic pictures of Costello, in the sense that it reveals the persona he uses in his songs. He's both hero and anti-hero: the 'tec's integrity and self-reliance are admirable, and we're on his side throughout the film, yet somehow we don't want to identify with him too strongly, for his honesty is too ruthless for comfort and we know that by the time the credits roll round at the end he'll be alone. He'll probably get involved with a woman in the course of the movie, but a parting scene is sure to feature in the last reel, charged with emotion on her side, laconic on his. The detective in the *film noir*, where the whole world seems to be in the grip of amoral thugs, is a perfect representative for Costello: true to himself, shrewd and a loner.

The sleeve's images illuminate the opening song, 'Clubland'. It's set in a nightclub peopled by characters straight out of a *film noir*, and has no first person narrator, which gives the impression that the 'story' is being told by someone sitting at one of the side tables who's watching with grim satisfaction but not getting involved himself, like a 'tec. The setting is a return trip to the seedy and shady world of *This Year's Model*, especially 'Pump It Up'. But whereas in the earlier song Costello is chiefly concerned with clubs as a symbol of a meaningless existence, and with denigrating their denizens, in 'Clubland' his venom is directed more towards those people who corruptly profit from them.

Throughout the song there is a strong emphasis on illegality; the opening line, for example, mentions 'back-handers', and there are many similar words and phrases. The effect of this is to evoke a world of gangster movies, where the people in charge are fairly blatantly crooked. And sharp practice is not their only method of doing business: the beginning of the second verse makes it clear that they're not slow to use violence to persuade their more tardy customers. The 'Clubland' video makes this point well with its images of threatening bouncers patrolling the club. They might be wearing dinner-jackets, but you only have to look at their soulless almost sneering faces to realise that you're not going to get any polite dinner-party conversation from them.

The verses are in B minor, a suitably dark and ominous key for their sinister overtones, but the chorus unexpectedly modulates to B major in a sudden impassioned outburst. It addresses ordinary people – us, the listeners – and asks rhetorically if we've ever been had. The primary meaning of this is, of course, to point out that we are being swindled, but there is also an appropriate sexual sense. To be 'had' implies being taken advantage of sexually, for only people who treat sex as a means of asserting their imagined dominance by temporarily possessing someone's body use this term. This highlights the song's subtext: the exploitation of sex. For example, the end of the second verse has a reference to the club's customers being abandoned 'halfway to bliss', which perhaps suggests the way in which striptease promises infinite satisfaction but then casually drops the unfulfilled punters. Even supposedly consummated sex in such an atmosphere is presumably a far from satisfying experience. Like Chinese food, it might satiate you for a short time, but before long you realise the insubstantiality of what you've had and you want more. It's this desire the club plays on to attract clientele.

On *Trust* the middle loses the importance it had on the previous two albums, but 'Clubland' has one of Costello's wittiest. The two lines are a kind of extended pun on 'outskirts' (suburbs/women's clothing). The first implies that the police are almost as corruptible as the crooks, as in 'Less Than Zero' and indeed *film noir*. The second returns to the crude groping sexuality which such clubs spring from and foster. Their subterranean gloom is a fitting setting for dark deeds and couplings about as meaningful as those of rabbits in a warren.

So 'Clubland' is the latest variation on Costello's perennial theme of the exploitation of the gullible by the callous. The last verse's fleeting references to unemployment make it clear that the clubs in question are not catering for the rich and trendy, but for ordinary people who are desperate for a little glamour, however tacky, to enliven their prosaic lives. Naturally they don't get it, or are at best offered only tantalising glimpses. The nightclubs can be seen as a metaphor for Britain of the 1980s, because as in 'Opportunity' glittering prizes are dangled before eager eyes, only to be snatched away again. The song is half contemptuous because people are so easily taken in, and half compassionate, because they're patently no match for the commissars of clubland. Thus the song provides a panoramic view of society, from the profiteers to the punters, and the deftness with which Costello paints his broad canvas puts 'Clubland' among his dozen or so best songs.

The title of 'Lovers Walk', like that of 'Girls Talk', shows Costello to be almost congenitally incapable of using a common phrase without somehow tinkering with it to make it new. Both these titles sound like much used phrases, but as we listen to the songs we realise that they are being used instead as statements. So what at first seem to be unremarkable phrases, even clichés, are transformed and we suddenly have to listen to them with fresh ears. These are only fairly mundane examples of Costello's constant, some would say obsessive, juggling with words. His songs, especially in the great middle period of which *Trust* forms a part, are full of word-play, and this is one of their great delights.

I've allowed myself to become diverted because there's not a great deal to say about 'Lovers Walk' itself. It's possibly Costello's simplest song, both lyrically and musically, and appears more like a sketch or doodle than the varnished masterpiece of 'Clubland'. The words are virtually a list with little sense of progression; a litany of despair. Most of his songs about the agonies of love imply that one partner triumphs over the other, but here both are broken. He even goes so far as to state that this is 'no one's fault', a much more humane and mature attitude to take than the acrid accusations of many earlier songs.

The first two songs are about observation rather than direct experience, but the next song is very definitely one in which the first person narrator is himself involved. Costello is no longer writing as a private eye, but as 'I'. 'You'll Never Be A Man' is a song in which the narrator has painfully confused emotions for a woman. It begins with a crudely simple tune, and the words too are distinctly squalid and sadistic, for they are reminiscent of the songs on *Get Happy!!* that involve violence against women. So far the song is not promising, but the end of the verses is regenerating. The aggression is temporarily set aside as the music becomes much more fluid, and the tone more benign, as he asks her to 'find the fake' in him. This clearly implies that the earlier brutality is an attempt to hide 'weak' emotions behind a macho façade, and the narrator is pleading for honesty and tenderness.

This ambivalence becomes even more obvious in the chorus. It's difficult to decide whether the chorus is affectionate or scornful. To tell her that she'll 'never be a man' could be a gentle reminder, but alternatively it could be a sneer indicating that however hard she tries to be one of the boys she'll never make it. This intentional ambiguity enriches the whole song, reinforcing the narrator's bewilderment and anguish.

The chorus veers between further snide remarks (including the apparently unequivocal statement that he'd kill her if he could, which if taken at face value is the most extreme expression of personal violence in any of Costello's songs) and what amount to admissions that he has only a very tentative grip on his own equilibrium. The last line, for example, and the protracted 'Oh' that follows it, show him doubting his ability to keep his head above water at all. The contrast between vehement contempt and disquietude is emphasised by one of Costello's most effective and affecting key changes. The beginnings of the verses and chorus are in A, but halfway through they lift a tone and a half to C.

The effect is magical: the crass brutality is left behind (or below) and we are in a higher frame of mind. Here the narrator no longer feels the need to brashly strut, but can admit his humanity and need for affection. 'You'll Never Be A Man' is not unlike 'Human Torch' in its juxtaposition of violence and tenderness, and while it's not a great song it's one I find particularly moving.

The early albums identify the media as a special target for invective, and the battle is rejoined in 'Pretty Words'. This is, in part, an attack on the cheaper newspapers, which is combined with a depiction of a stale personal relationship to form a powerful piece of cynicism about the corruption and debasement of language. This is presumably a subject close to Costello's heart, and certainly close to his art, since he is evidently concerned with the considered use of language, and the result is one of *Trust*'s most interesting songs.

The first verse shows the narrator struggling to communicate with his partner, and the second (note, though, that this is one of the few songs in which two verses are sung successively, without the chorus coming between them) puts this relationship in its social context. Other people in this song are like the inhabitants of clubland, louts and wide-boys. Some of them are gloating over pornographic magazines, which both establishes their grossness and begins to influence the listener against the press. The first time the chorus is sung the 'pretty words', which are now almost meaningless, are presumably the words that pass between the narrator and his partner. He does his best to not be affected by them, because he realises that their prettiness is merely superficial, thinly disguising the lack of true feeling. Consequently the chorus ends with a dismissive sneer at the woman's shallowness.

The third and fourth verses, however, don't directly refer to her at all. Instead the third offers some snapshots of a world in disarray, and the fourth begins the attack on the press in earnest. The narrator buys a newspaper, and is horrified to find that it contains 'just cartoons and titter-tatter'. The tabloid papers relentlessly trivialise the news, filling their pages with horribly hearty frivolity and gossip about soap opera stars. They can hardly be called newspapers at all, their coverage of world events not getting exactly high priority in their pages unless some sex scandal trivia is involved. They're more like adult comics, though perhaps 'adult' is a misnomer here. Costello is concerned in particular with the way in which they degrade language, forcing all sentences

79

into a straitjacket of tabloidspeak clichés. Everything is sensationalised: fires are 'blazes' or 'infernos', any journey, however leisurely, to help someone becomes a 'mercy dash'. The result is that subtle nuances of language are banished, and all events can be neutered with a blanket word or phrase that reduces everything to the same level of banality. Costello commented on this in an interview in *Time Out* in 1983: 'The *Sun* is heading for a time when people will only recognise symbols, like the little ones they have for the weather. For them the perfect way of describing a nuclear attack would be to have a little picture of St Paul's and then a mushroom cloud above it.' A devastating comment. (Incidentally, I can't resist recording my favourite *Sun* headline, which I assure you is genuine, which must have appeared in 1982: 'My Sex Mad Wife's Lust For Snooker Star Willie.' I always thought they used cues, but there you are.)

So when the chorus is repeated its implications are different. Now, instead of berating the woman for her insincerity, it laments the way in which words are deprived of their power. Failures of communication have been a theme of Costello's songs since 'Radio Sweetheart', but here the suggestion is that the lines have fallen not just between one man and one woman, but everywhere. The fear expressed in the song is that language is being so corrupted that it's becoming meaningless, and that sooner or later we won't be able to express ourselves except in the simplest and blandest terms. I've already referred to *Nineteen Eighty-Four* when discussing 'Green Shirt', and Orwell's invention of 'Newspeak', a language so simple that the expression of original ideas or genuine feelings is all but impossible, comes to mind here. There's no hint in the song that the debasement of language is a deliberate conspiracy to suppress individuality, as it is in the book, but nevertheless the result is the same. 'Pretty Words' is quite an achievement: not many songwriters would even attempt to deal with this subject, and to put it so succinctly and memorably is remarkable.

'Strict Time', like 'Lovers Walk', gives the impression of being unfinished, a doodle rather than a fully worked out idea. Nevertheless it's got some good lines, and the perky piano riff makes it worth listening to. In it we descend once more into clubland, where the men and women enact their mating rituals. The general drift of the song is that the behaviour of people in such surroundings is hardly motivated by free will, but is dictated by set patterns.

The title 'Strict Time', like that of 'The Beat', is a musical metaphor, implying that despite the illusion of carefree and spontaneous behaviour everyone acts in accordance with a rigid rule-book. Particular records demand that listeners dance in certain ways; they join in the 'audience participation' conducted by a DJ; seductions follow familiar routines. The club's customers sound like a flock of libidinous zombies. In the first line the narrator describes himself as a ventriloquist's dummy, incapable of independent movement; throughout the song runs the sense of being trapped in a robotic nightmare. The song offers no hope of escape; the best the narrator can do is, in the chorus, to advise us to keep a stiff upper lip. Stoical endurance is a new weapon in Costello's anti-reality armoury.

'Luxembourg' is terrifically enjoyable, musically verging on pastiche – Elvis the C sings Elvis the P rockabilly style. It's full of energy and dash – one of those songs where there's a paradoxical contrast between the depressing (though witty) lyric and the sheer joy of the music. It deals with a subject not previously employed by Costello, the tourist trade, though he uses this subject for a familiar assault on modern life.

The chorus is not very specific, but enough clues are given to leave the impression that the events described in the verses take place on a guided coach tour around Europe. The tourists pay no attention to the sights they're supposed to be seeing, being shepherded uncomprehendingly around art galleries and cathedrals. Why do they go on such trips in the first place? Presumably for the various comically awful sexual shenanigans that splutter into life in the hotel rooms in the evenings. Both men and women behave like predators, trying to outmanoeuvre each other, and in the middle these relationships are seen in distinctly sinister terms. Clubland is uprooted from its featureless buildings in suburbia and sent on a saturnalian trip.

Trust is an album peculiarly rich in warnings, and 'Watch Your Step' is the most sustained example of this trend. It's hard to say precisely what the warning is, except that it counsels us not to overstep the mark, to be cautious and wary. This is consistent with Costello's frequently expressed desire that we do not allow ourselves to be tricked and exploited, though this desire is usually mixed with disgust as he assumes that his advice won't be heeded. The first line of the song consists of another injunction, to be silent, like that in 'Strict Time', so it seems that the best policy to adopt in life is to be like a laconic, distanced detective.

'Watch Your Step' is set mostly among the young male customers of a pub. The warning is addressed predominantly to them, and Costello's breathy vocals make it sound particularly intimate and threatening. The narrator's attitude to the men is disdainful: he focuses in particular on their drink-inspired delusions and violence, painting a pretty unappealing picture of them. The second chorus, for example, evokes their boozy cama-raderie and their cheerful approval of bar-room fights, and the last verse begins with their early evening hopes of sexual success, but shows how they end up, sublimating their desires with drink and acts of petty vandalism. However, while it's true that disdain for their mindless behaviour is uppermost in the song, there is an undercurrent of sympathy. There are some hints that they are being manipulated, like the customers in 'Clubland', for the benefit of the powerful. Thus the drinkers cannot be entirely blamed for their behaviour, as they are perhaps being deliberately kept in this semi-animal condition. It's 'good for business' for them to be so.

The last lines, sung with an audible sneer, end the song with an extremely striking image reminding us of the inevitable fact of death. This suddenly puts all the previous incidents into perspec-tive: the youths' search for pleasure, and the shadowy schemers' string-pulling, are merely insignificant and vain gestures that ulti-mately signify nothing. This is a characteristically Costellian touch, throwing a veil of profound fatalism over the whole song. In the end, then, 'Watch Your Step' is more than another disgusted dissection of lives that are full of sound and fury but otherwise cavernously empty. Its broodingly soulful intensity is like a requiem for all vain wishes.

So side one ends ambivalently, with compassion struggling with contempt, and side two begins similarly, though at last sympathy and even tenderness begin to get the upper hand. 'New Lace Sleeves' is another of *Trust*'s outstanding songs; it's a kind of companion piece to 'Pretty Words', setting a personal relationship (dealt with in the chorus) in its social context (the subject of the verses), and considering deceptions.

Despite its eventual warmth it begins dryly and cynically enough with a description of a couple waking in bed, probably after a 'one-night stand'. It seems that neither partner especially desired this, but as in 'Strict Time' once the initial moves have been made they are virtually destined to follow the steps of the ritual dance all the way to the bedroom. The second verse places the couple among the Martini set, and although the narrator envies their leisured and relatively carefree lives it's clear that he regards them as worthless drones.

Juxtaposed with this emotional sterility is the chorus, addressed to 'you', who is presumably the narrator's lover. The transition from the third person of the verses to the second person at once brings a sense of intimacy, and although he's torn between scorn and affection (as in 'You'll Never Be A Man') he's now sorrowful rather than accusatory. He's saddened by the ease with which she's taken in by all the half-truths she's fed by people anxious to exploit her. The first verse contains passing references to the press, and, as we've seen before, in Costello's view the press's devotion to the truth is not total, so we're back with the familiar subject of the media's deliberate manipulation of the gullible. It's not quite that simple on this occasion, however, because she seems to almost realise that she is being lied to and exploited, and yet still she allows herself to go along with it. The narrator finds this doublethink hard to accept, and his bewilderment is expressed in the painfully beautiful melisma on the word 'believe'. But despite his awareness of her naivety, he can't help being moved by her innocence and vulnerability, and the last line, where he concedes that the 'new lace sleeves' she's rather girlishly proud of are actually quite fetching, is sung with real feeling. It would be going too far to describe 'New Lace Sleeves' as a love song, but at least it does admit the possibility of love, and the hesitant little tune (with no phrases longer than two bars) perfectly captures this sense of gingerly stepping into potentially dangerous territory. It's certainly one of Costello's most human songs.

'From A Whisper To A Scream' was one of the two tracks from *Trust* to be released as a single in the UK, the other being 'Clubland'; (the choice in the USA was 'Watch Your Step'). With so many excellent songs on the album it seems an odd one to hit upon, and indeed it was almost completely ignored by the record-buying public and failed to make any impression at all on the charts. It didn't deserve this ignominious fate, for while it's some way from Costello's best it's pleasingly punchy, and is of added interest as it features the aggressive guitar work of Martin Belmont and a vocal duet with Glenn Tilbrook of Squeeze, (whose excellent album *East Side Story*, released a few months after *Trust*, was co-produced by Costello).

The lyric is one of several on the album that seem unfinished: a collection of jottings rather than a polished statement. The second verse is, perhaps, the most interesting. It's set in a pub or similar place where the customers are entrenched in a protracted drinking session, thus reminding us of similar scenes in 'Clubland' and 'Watch Your Step'. The consumption could even be a symbol of consumerism itself, which debilitates customers as alcohol does and turns them into addicts. So in the chorus there's an agonised but unspecific plea to be rescued and released from this trap, the two voices rising together in an inarticulate but eloquent SOS. If 'From A Whisper To A Scream' is a warning about the perils of consumerism then the customers can hardly be blamed for taking its message to heart and refraining from consuming this particular record.

'Different Finger' takes up where 'Stranger In The House' left off. It's another pastiche country song, beautifully done as far as the limits of this particular genre allow. The song is tucked away in probably the least conspicuous place on any album, the middle of side two, but the nonchalant mastery with which Costello handles this relatively unfamiliar style should be noticed. The lyric is exceptionally straightforward and so requires little comment, but I'll point out, in the first verse, yet another reference to being watched, and at the end, a child-like longing for security. It's also curious to note that this is the first song by Costello to be about a specifically adulterous affair: in the earlier songs there's no definite suggestion that either partner is married. Consequently guilt is for obvious reasons a dominant emotion in 'Different Finger'.

Violence against women is a fairly prominent theme on *Get Happy!!* and Costello revisits the subject in 'White Knuckles'. Several of the songs from the previous album, 'Human Touch' for example, involve the narrator hitting his partner, and while the album as a whole is against violence it's still rather worrying that in some individual songs Costello should write in the first person about wife-beating. 'White Knuckles', like 'Beaten To The Punch', is a kind of antidote to these songs, because it is a denunciation of an immature man who uses violence against his partner. It does have a first person narrator, but he plays no part in it except that of aghast observer.

The relationship is indeed a horrifying one. The man is habitually aggressive to the woman on the slightest pretext, for example when she whispers to him in public, thus making him feel unmanly, and he presumably has to later establish his virility by knocking her around a bit. Although he is monstrous and revolting, Costello fills in enough social background to make this understandable, though certainly not excusable. It's clear that the man has been brought up in a world where feelings are hardly admitted, and where brash machismo is the standard male stance. Consequently he is bemused by kissing, for example, and probably is equally uncomprehending of all expressions of affection. Given this it's hardly surprising that he behaves as he does, though this doesn't prevent the narrator and listener being shocked. What's more, the pressures of consumerism appear again in the shape of a reference to the 'never-never', hire purchase, and from this it's possible to guess that another cause of violence is finance. The couple have perhaps over-committed themselves in pursuit of a fantasy, an advertisement-induced lifestyle, and can't keep up with the payments. His frustration at not being able to attain the goodies spotlighted all around him is vented in violence. It's next to impossible to feel any sympathy for him, but he's a victim nonetheless.

Possibly the most depressing aspect of the song is the apparent submission of the woman. Despite the warnings of other women (in the coda) her tragedy is that she can't imagine any other way of life. She is trapped, as securely as a bird in a cage, by her own lack of expectations. 'White Knuckles' is one of the bleakest of all Costello's songs; both lyrically and musically it's like a vast expanse of featureless tundra stretching to and beyond the horizon.

This impression of an infinity of suffering is reinforced by the next song, 'Shot With His Own Gun', a study of an equally stale relationship. Indeed, it could almost be the same relationship as that described in 'White Knuckles', except that now violence is only vaguely hinted at rather than being the crux of the whole song. The lyric of 'Shot With His Own Gun' is one of Costello's most controlled and consistent, with every line contributing to the effect. The music is appropriately sparse, the recording featuring only Costello's voice and Nieve's piano. This is the first time that such a minimal arrangement has been used, (except on the exquisite live recording of 'Accidents Will Happen' on the

'Live At The Hollywood High' EP), and the result is starkly beautiful.

As in the previous song, Costello's sympathy is with the woman, addressed with the relatively intimate 'you' while the man is referred to more distantly in the third person. The first verse makes it clear that her marriage has not at all lived up to her starry-eyed expectations. So many people marry believing it will end their problems, whereas in fact it can be the beginning of new and more awkward ones. Marriage isn't a word, it's a sentence, as the saying goes. Her husband quickly proves to be coldly salacious and uncommunicative. Their relationship rapidly crumbles, their sex life, initially an excitement for them both, decays, leaving them unfulfilled, and he resorts to drink. Although, as I've said, there are no specific references to violence, it's well known that drunkenness is one of the main causes of wife-beating, so perhaps this is her eventual fate. All that's left for her now is 'playing house'; she has to act out a sham as the real thing eludes her.

'White Knuckles' and 'Shot With His Own Gun' are significant milestones in Costello's career. The very early songs usually show the woman getting the upper hand, but this gradually changes until the man is just as likely to be the top dog, in which case he often relishes his triumph over her with sneers. Take the previous album's 'B Movie'. Here the man, despite the weakness implicit in the last verse's last line, at least superficially thoroughly enjoys telling his partner how insignificant she is. It's true that some previous songs show despicable men abusing women, 'This Year's Girl', for example, but generally the attitude of these songs is to despise the women too for their gullibility. *Trust*, however, is a big step forward. At last women are portrayed with genuine sympathy, without routine cynicisms and brutalities. 'White Knuckles' and 'Own Gun' in particular, while certainly not offering any solutions, at least try to understand why relationships fail, rather than simply hitting out verbally and physically. Partly for this reason, 'Shot With His Own Gun', like the not dissimilar 'Accidents Will Happen', is one of Costello's most moving songs.

After the two previous depressing songs Costello offers us one of his rare excursions into something approaching frivolity. 'Fish 'n 'Chip Paper' is delightful if rather disconnected, a collage of images, their only apparent connection being that they are all wry reflections on modern life. We're given glimpses of a world governed by Sod's Law, where something always ruins potential enjoyment. But this is all done without bitterness, and the tone of the song is gently shoulder-shrugging at the almost comic absurdity of life. This mood is perfectly complemented by the jaunty guitar and organ solos – the musicians are having fun pure and simple for perhaps the first time on the album. The last line of the chorus 'Yesterday's news is tomorrow's fish'n'chip paper', is not only a neat saying (how long before it appears in some book of aphorisms?), but also reminds us of *Trust*'s concern with the press, as well as bringing to the fore Costello's recurrent theme of time and transience. But despite these oblique glances at serious issues 'Fish'n'Chip Paper' provides some welcome light relief.

Trust is the first of Costello's albums to end with one of its best songs. In fact 'Big Sister's Clothes' is a great song; virtually every line is worthy of quotation; it's crammed like an overfull suitcase with puns, observations, incisive phrases, wisdom. Its high quality is partly the result of its combination of the best features of the three previous songs – the insight and sympathy of 'White Knuckles' and 'Shot With His Own Gun', and the rueful and understated tone of 'Fish'n'Chip Paper'. Its subject matter, sterile relationships, is very familiar, but the sadly amused style sets the song apart.

The first verse deals with the ways in which people are unsuspectingly lead into marriage. Their wide-eyed innocence and artless naivety cause them to see only the attractions and none of the pitfalls. They blindly trust in the power of love, and, as is bound to happen when the blind lead the blind, they end up falling into ditches. The verses are in major keys, E modulating halfway through to G (incidentally, key changes rising a tone and a half seem to especially appeal to Costello – he uses them in several songs), but the chorus is in E minor. This immediately changes the mood from nearly cynical to regretfully contemplative. Costello quietly laments people's impetuous eagerness to take on the responsibilities of adulthood before they're ready for them. In particular they rush into marriage, oblivious of the consequences, with results exposed in, for example, 'Shot With His Own Gun'. The last line of the chorus, pointing out how young girls are always anxious to grow up before their time, is perhaps not as instantly memorable as that of 'Fish'n'Chip Paper', but is nevertheless a superb image. Most of us have seen small girls proudly sporting their 'big sister's clothes', perhaps heavily and amateurishly made up too, unaware of how ludicrous they really appear. This homely metaphor impresses on us the equally ludicrous, but also tragic, consequences of leaping into adulthood without looking.

The middle, back in roguish rhythm and major key, remarks on how widespread love and lust are, and, in the album's latest and last reference to the press, how keen the media are to make capital out of them. The second verse reverts to another of Costello's favourite themes, sex described in such a way as to make it seem distasteful. All this is done with a lightness of touch that's very different from the fulminations to be found on earlier albums. There are even traces of the hell-fire preacher in a few songs, but 'Big Sister's Clothes' is much less condemnatory and more compassionate. *My Aim Is True* ends with bitter cynicism, *This Year's Model* and *Armed Forces* with fearful warnings, *Get Happy!!* with the narrator on the rack, but *Trust* concludes with nothing like as much pomp, with a gentle, almost wistful, understatement.

'Big Sister's Clothes' is undoubtedly one of Costello's best songs, so it's surprising to note that in a 1984 interview he claimed to have written it before his recording career had started, though he didn't explain why it hadn't been recorded earlier. Some light was thrown on this matter when a song called 'Big Sister' was released as part of the B-side of 'You Little Fool' in 1982. The lyric of the verses and middle are the same as those of 'Big Sister's Clothes', but the chorus is entirely different, as is all the music. This chorus contains a direct reference to Orwell's famous parody of a totalitarian slogan in *Nineteen Eighty-Four*, 'Big Brother Is Watching You', thus incidentally proving that Costello is familiar with the book at least by repute. This transforms the song into an attack on women, like 'Miracle Man', accusing them of manipulating men for their own selfish ends. 'Big Sister', unlike any other song released in 1982, was produced by Nick Lowe, who also produced *Trust*, with the single significant exception of 'Big Sister's Clothes' which Costello produced himself. From this evidence it's my guess that 'Big Sister' is the original song and was recorded for inclusion on *Trust*, but that Costello realised that, despite many wonderful lines, as it was it was retrogressive. So he ditched the offending chorus, wrote a new one, thus making the song far more mature, and composed new music to fit its now rueful mood. This is only my guess, but if I'm right it demonstrates what a careful craftsman Costello is, honing and refining till he gets it right.

And it's my contention that on *Trust* as a whole he does get it more or less right. This doesn't seem to be a popular view: I know fans of Costello who regard it as a hotch-potch of good and bad jumbled up together. I admit that some songs are sketchy, and that stylistically it's his most varied album except possibly *Armed Forces* (which has an obvious theme running through the lyrics to unify it, which *Trust* lacks). But variety is an asset, especially when it's built around a central idea, as I hope to show it is in *Trust*. The 1981 songs lack the sheer fecundity of the 1980 vintage, but there are still inspirations fizzing and bubbling and popping up all over the place, and I regard *Trust* as one of Costello's very best albums.

If you listen carefully to the lyrics, one of the first things that strikes you is that they are much less personal than previously. If you conducted a statistical survey of the first four albums (which I have no intention of actually doing) you would probably find that a large majority of the songs are partly or entirely about the relationship between one man and one woman (not necessarily the same man and woman in different songs, of course). But on *Trust* only about half fit into this category, though a couple of others are about personal relationships in general, so there's a subtle but significant shift of emphasis.

Furthermore, the primacy of the first person narrator has been undermined. Before *Trust* the vast majority of songs have a narrator, and in most of them, personal and public alike, he is directly involved in the action. The early Costello generally writes from the inside, and the result is powerful, passionate and exhausting. This is not to say that the songs are autobiographical – perhaps they are, perhaps they aren't – but he imagines himself very vividly into the situations and enacts them as it were in front of an audience. The effect is sometimes almost embarrassingly intimate, but the listener can hardly fail to become involved. Writing in the first person Costello often lets feelings boil over, rage and disgust usually frothing right over the sides of the cauldron and mixing with the flames to produce much steam and noise. The fury of the performance hardly lets gentler emotions get a look-in at all. While it's true that there are still substantial traces of this compositional technique on *Trust* ('From A Whisper To A Scream', for example), quite a few of the songs are now written from the outside rather than the inside. Three of them have no first person narrator ('Clubland', 'Luxembourg' and 'Shot With His Own Gun') while another four have a narrator who's an observer rather than a participant ('Lovers Walk', 'Watch Your Step', 'White Knuckles' and 'Big Sister's Clothes'). The effect of this is to give a broader view as Costello steps back from the action. The songs tend now to be objective rather than subjective, giving a much clearer impression of the social background, more thoughtful, compassionate as well as passionate, and less concerned with personal axe-grinding.

One result of this is that most of the *Trust* songs are less melodramatic than many of their predecessors. The earlier songs are often about people in emotionally highly-charged situations, like pressure-cookers waiting to explode. The characters of the *Trust* songs, on the other hand, are generally in ordinary, dull situations. Compare 'Man Called Uncle' with 'Shot With His Own Gun', for example. Both songs are about unsatisfactory relationships, but the former is not only set partly in a sleazy bar and a bedroom, potentially dramatic locations, but also features several relatively sensational details, such as the woman checking through her handbag after a night with her lover. The song simmers and steams. The latter song, however, describes a much more prosaic situation, a marriage that's gone off the boil. The atmosphere is no longer torrid, but merely dreary. Both ways of approaching writing a song have their merits (though I should imagine that it's extremely difficult to write about dreary subjects without ending up with dreary songs). The difference between them is something like that between a Hollywood Technicolour tearjerker and a gritty monochrome film full of social realism.

It would be nice to be able to report that this distance from his subjects gives Costello some grounds for optimism. Unfortunately this is not the case. Personal relationships are still seen as sources of dissatisfaction and worse, even though the songs make some attempt to be analytic and not just descriptive. The figure of the demanding disdainful woman on whom everything can be blamed has virtually disappeared; men are now more likely to find themselves accused. More importantly, *Trust* tends not to single out people who are supposedly at fault, but instead blames no one and everyone. Malevolent fate hangs over the album.

One of the causes of unhappy relationships, and one of the album's chief preoccupations, is immaturity. Many earlier songs exhibit this, intentionally or unintentionally ('I'm Not Angry', for example, with its pouting little-boyishness), and it has formed part of the subject of a few, such as 'The Beat'. But on *Trust* at least three songs, 'Watch Your Step', 'White Knuckles' and of course the album's clinching 'Big Sister's Clothes', are largely about immaturity and its consequences. Several others contain passing allusions to it. You can hardly blame someone for being immature: it's not at all easy to know who is responsible, if anyone. Perhaps these permanent or at any rate protracted adolescences are the result of social, economic and emotional suppression – if people are denied power they can't learn to use it wisely. This thought neatly links together the personal and public songs.

The politics of *Trust* are familiar in their general outline: a few people deliberately keep everyone else in a state of ignorance so that the minority can exploit and profit from the majority. This theme can be clearly seen in 'Clubland', for example. But there's another shift of emphasis. Previously the press has been just one of several targets for Costello's spleen, but now it's singled out for sustained attack. 'Pretty Words' is the key instance of this, but several other songs contain passing though specific references to the papers ('Watch Your Step','New Lace Sleeves', 'Own Gun', 'Fish'n'Chip Paper' and 'Big Sister's Clothes'). We are thus frequently reminded of what amounts to the popular newspapers' campaign of misinformation. The general drift of the songs is that the tabloids propagate a false view of the world, not necessarily by printing definite lies, but by trivialising, glossing over and ignoring serious issues. They give the impression that the world is like a huge Butlin's holiday camp. Uncritical readers of the *Sun* (if such benighted creatures really exist) must get the impression that the only important things in life are sex, soap opera, royalty and sport. Their critical faculties remain uneducated, and consequently they have little chance of being able to see through the way they're being manipulated. They believe in the simplistic stories they're fed (hence presumably the title *Trust*) and become all the more pliable and gullible. In many earlier songs Costello's reaction to the deception of the media is to fall into paroxysms of rage, as in 'Radio Radio', but now his response is, if still angry, much more measured, almost resigned.

'Measured' and 'resigned' are quite good words with which to sum up *Trust*. Costello's vocal performance, and the playing of the Attractions, are very fine indeed. The frenetic anxiety of *Get Happy!!* has largely dissipated and instead we hear how well the musicians can cope with a wide variety of styles. It's difficult to write about musical performances without using increasingly pretentious metaphors, so I'll just list a few of the highlights: Nieve's piano solo in 'Clubland', Bruce Thomas's bass in 'From A Whisper To A Scream', Pete Thomas's drums in 'New Lace Sleeves', and Costello's vocals in 'You'll Never Be A Man'. There are no fireworks, no theatrics, just superbly controlled musicianship. *Trust* is in almost every respect an impeccable album. Why it was commercially no more than marginally successful must rank as one of the great unsolved mysteries of our time, along with why at jazz concerts the drum solos get the most enthusiastic applause.

The fourteen songs on the album were the only original ones to be released in 1981, but one other song seems to have been recorded during the *Trust* sessions, though not released until 1986 (on the B-side of the 12-inch version of 'Tokyo Storm Warning'). This is 'Black Sails In The Sunset', a rather mysterious song, dominated, like many of this period, by Nieve's piano. I take it to be another *memento mori*, a reminder of death. Despite its gruesome subject, it's a good song and deserves to be better known. Heaven knows why it was kept under wraps for so long. (I sometimes toy with the idea that Costello is in some ways a rock version of the poet Philip Larkin, and this song contains the only verbal echo that I've spotted. In a poem first published in 1955 Larkin describes death as 'a black-sailed unfamiliar'. This might or might not be the source of Costello's 'black sails in the sunset'.)

Fifteen songs in one year, though not as remarkable as the twenty-four of 1980, would make many musicians feel entitled to p t their feet up for a while. Costello's feet refused to remain in slippers for too long, however, and itched to find themselves in some cowboy boots. So urged on by his extremities he recorded a whole new album just a few months after the release of *Trust*. This was *Almost Blue*, a collection of country songs, recorded in, where else, Nashville. Costello's interest in country music had been evident since the very early 'Radio Sweetheart', but even so I can remember the surprise, shock even, I felt when I first heard about this project. The pressure was obviously too much for him and he'd finally flipped his lid (maybe the pressure cooker valve was faulty). I knew almost nothing about country music (and know only a little more now) but regarded it as musically bumpkinish and lyrically the twentieth century equivalent of mawkish Victorian parlour ballads. So when I eventually heard *Almost Blue* (after scorning buying it) I was taken aback to find that I rather liked it. I'm not going to discuss it in any detail since the songs on it aren't written by Costello, but while some of them sail pretty close to being kitsch, 'Success', for example, the commitment of the performances carry them through. *Almost Blue* is a brave experiment, and a successful one.

Several other country songs recorded during the same sessions surfaced on B-sides, but one recorded live in 1979, released as the B-side of 'Sweet Dreams', is my favourite. This is 'Psycho', a song loosely based on the Hitchcock film and sung in the persona of a Norman Bates-like figure. I'm not sure whether it was written seriously or as a send up, and Costello's performance leaves the same doubt, but nevertheless the result is hilarious. It's so gloriously over the top that it makes Iron Maiden sound like masters of understatement. Costello surely intends this to be funny, but if not we can be grateful that for once his innate sense of good taste has deserted him.

93

7

'Imperial Bedroom'

In one way *Trust* marked the end of an era, in that it was the last Costello album to be produced by Nick Lowe for five years. *Almost Blue* was produced by the veteran Nashville musician Billy Sherrill, and according to its sleeve *Imperial Bedroom* was 'Produced by Geoff Emerick from an original idea by Elvis Costello'. Lowe's self-effacing merits as a producer should be recognised; he allows the songs to speak for themselves by using only the absolute minimum studio trickery. Costello's vocals are quite often double or even treble tracked, and Nieve sometimes takes advantage of technology to play more than one keyboard instrument at a time, but otherwise there's not much that couldn't be performed live on stage by Costello and the Attractions. There's certainly a lot to be said for this uncomplicated no-nonsense approach – it makes the songs sound spontaneous and immediate, and, after all, most of them are good enough not to need any distracting studio frills. Indeed, many are so strong that they can survive, even benefit from, the most basic, unadorned performances, as Costello proved in his solo concerts of 1984 and 85 when his vocals were accompanied by only his scratchy guitar work. And there can't be too many rock songwriters who'd relish giving their songs such stark, almost indecent exposure.

There's nothing remotely stark about the production of *Imperial Bedroom*. Lowe's departure signalled the end, at least temporarily, of such simplicity, and ushered in a period of rococo elaboration, of baroque and roll. Many people have misgivings about this, feeling that the numerous overdubs and multi-trackings, and the introduction of extraneous instruments (including a full orchestra), obscure rather than illuminate the songs. Mick St Michael, for example, in his biography of Costello, is quite scathing about the album's production, claiming that it sounds like 'the schoolboy who had the pick of the sweetshop', referring of course to Costello's apparently gleeful toying with all the studio's gadgets once Mr Lowe the teacher's back was turned. There's certainly some truth in this view, and I'm glad none of the other albums were produced like this. Several of the songs, 'Shabby Doll' for example, sound much better live – more direct and powerful – than they do on the record. One the other hand, though, some of the *Imperial Bedroom* songs are unusually complex and so seem suited to multilayered productions. What's more, some benefit from being given a sense of grandeur, an epic quality, though it has to be admitted that at times it's in danger of crumbling into mere grandiosity. But whatever your opinion of the production, *Imperial Bedroom* remains a collection of high quality songs.

The opening track, 'Beyond Belief', is one of the complex songs to which I've just referred. It's hard to pin it down and say precisely what it's about – there are so many ideas and characters swirling around in it that it's like an hallucination, or perhaps a nightmare. This lack of focus could be partly the result of its disjointed composition (according to St Michael it underwent unusually radical revision during its recording), but whatever the cause it's dizzily disorientating. The multi-tracked vocals weave in and out of each other like conversations running around a large room, and the effect is, as Costello himself said, 'to suggest that there [is] more than one attitude going on inside the songs'. Most earlier songs have a narrator who sings, so to speak, from the same position throughout the song. But in 'Beyond Belief' it seems as if he is wandering around, firing off thoughts as they occur to him in no particular order, rambling out a stream of consciousness. (The song contains a couple of references to drinking, so a less literary explanation of its hazy nature could be that the narrator is simply pissed.)

'Beyond Belief' is fundamentally a jaundiced and horror-struck meditation on the state of the world. The opening couplet serves as a kind of prelude to the album as a whole: it reminds us that people generally don't learn from their mistakes. A study of the past reveals that problems are always vainly countered with pomposities and naiveties, and that consequently they're often not solved. Infuriatingly, humankind goes on repeating the same old failures again and again. As someone has said, the only thing we learn from history is that we don't learn from history. This goes for our own everyday lives too: we get ourselves into the same old messes time after time. The songs on *Imperial Bedroom* are full of mistakes that haven't been learnt from, and descriptions of the messes people make of their lives.

The type of woman who made her first appearance in 'Miracle Man' was virtually absent from *Trust*, but she now makes her re-entry. As before she's two-faced, malicious, coldly calculating, and desirable. In the coda the narrator realises that if he attempts to engage with her and the rest of the cruel world he's going to get hurt. There was a time when he was attracted by the supposed glamour of the rejected lover, the struggling artist, and so on, but he's through that stage now and is appalled at the prospect of having to act out these parts. This is like a recantation of Costello's attitude on previous albums: before he almost relished the position of outsider, and certainly he explored its various possibilities with something approaching dedication. But in 'Beyond Belief' he seems to be stating his intention of no longer being content to be simply a cynical observer, but playing a more active and more positive role.

What gives 'Beyond Belief' some kind of coherence and unity is the music. Apart from the middle the whole song is founded on a simple chord sequence – DGDF – around which Costello's voices work beautiful variations. The melody is extremely fluid; in fact phrases are rarely repeated, which gives an appropriate sense of musing aloud.

'Tears Before Bedtime' returns to the marital claustrophobia of many of the *Get Happy!!* songs. (It's true that *Trust* also dealt with this situation, but from the point of view of an observer, whereas 'Tears Before Bedtime' has a narrator very much involved in the action.) This is a subject more than adequately dealt with before, and the lyric adds little if anything new to our under-standing of how or why such relationships fail. Nevertheless, it unrelentingly piles up details of discord and is a convincing enough study.

In one respect 'Shabby Doll' is also a retrogressive song, in that the coquette, the teasing woman, makes another appearance. To call her a 'shabby doll' implies that once she was glamorous and chic but is now past her best, and also that she is intellectually and morally contemptible. We've met people like her before in many of the anti-fashionable society songs such as '(I Don't Want

To Go To) Chelsea'. It's not quite so simple this time, however, because the narrator, rather than assuming his superiority, also refers to himself as a 'shabby doll'. To complicate matters further the woman and narrator are not the only characters: someone is addressed as 'you', and an unnamed man enters the stage too. It's impossible to work out the relationship between them or who they are, and as in 'Beyond Belief' the effect is nightmarish. At times the song is virtually paranoic with its seedy underworld references. The music verges on the frantic, especially at the end with its strange demented cries. 'Shabby Doll' is distinctly uncomfortable.

The tale told by 'The Long Honeymoon' is also far from pleasant, but because it's presented in a much more conventional format it's far easier to cope with. Its closest relative is 'Shot With His Own Gun', for it's about a marriage that's gone stale, chiefly through the husband's fault. (I get the impression, though, that the couple in the earlier song are less well-off than the present pair.) The tune, with what sounds like a piano accordion accompanying it, is very beautiful: full of fragility and tenderness, the perfect match for the sad story.

The central character is the wife, sitting alone one evening in her (I imagine) expensively furnished house, waiting for her husband to return home from work. He's late, and Costello impressionistically sketches her fears as she wonders what he could be doing. There's not much doubt that he's having an affair, possibly with her best friend, and the chorus dwells on her solitude and sorrow. She jumped into marriage too quickly (as in 'Big Sister's Clothes') and now sees it crumbling around her. The last line of the chorus is psychologically extremely accurate: you might assume that if someone hurts you in this way then you'd resent and hate them, but most people's reaction to rejection is to love the person who's left them all the more fervently at least for a while. 'The Long Honeymoon' makes us feel real sympathy for the poor helpless woman.

'The Long Honeymoon' does not have a sung middle, but it does have an instrumental middle. (This is not the same as an ordinary instrumental where a soloist improvises around the chord sequence of another part of the song. By 'instrumental middle' I mean that the music is not a repetition of the verse or chorus.) This takes the form of one of Costello's fairly rare guitar solos, and the lovely melody evokes the woman's solitude and our powerlessness to help. In the coda the piano and brass take up the tune, and lead to the poignant conclusion. At the very end the brass adds a strange and unexpected chord, like an aural question mark. This chord (E with a diminished fifth) is startlingly remote from the tonic, so the effect is to create a feeling of homelessness and insecurity, echoing the wife's overwhelming sense of rejection.

After this subdued song there's a sudden outburst of cacophony – raucous guitar and terrified screaming – that shatters the sombre, thoughtful mood. This noise is a kind of bizarre fanfare announcing 'Man Out Of Time', one of Costello's most typical and best songs. It's also one of the songs that benefits most from the grand production, the Phil Spectorish wall-of-sound giving the impression of spaciousness and significance.

Three characters are identifiable: the central one is an unnamed man who seems to hold some kind of public position, such as the chair of a big company, then there's a woman, and then the narrator. The details remain obscure, and in some respects the song is as bewildering as 'Beyond Belief' or 'Shabby Doll', but the general scenario seems to be that the man has left the woman (possibly after having an affair with her), and the narrator is now pleading with her to love him instead. The verses are mostly concerned with denouncing the man, and Costello summons up all his considerable powers of invective to blast him away with great shock waves of scorn and revulsion. For example, he's said to have 'a mind like a sewer and a heart like a fridge' – a good example of Costello's skill in taking a cliché and twisting it to make it new and effective.

As well as attacking the man's character, the verses conjure up a vision of the sleazy London life he leads. We're back in the sinister underworld of 'Clubland', and although specific references are few, enough is said to give the impression of corruption undermining apparently decent society. For example, we're given a glimpse of 'the pretty things of Knightsbridge lying for a Minister of State'. Knightsbridge is superficially a smart and respectable part of London, so this line, with its simple but well executed pun on 'lying' (telling lies/lying down to have sex, but also with a faint echo of 'lying in wait' which makes the women in question sound predatory) exposes the amorality beneath the stylish veneer. The memories it brings of the Profumo affair, and other more recent sex scandals involving public figures, convince us that people in high places quite likely have something to hide. So the verses amount to a portrait of a society rotten to the core, infested by maggot-like opportunists.

So far the subject matter is relatively routine, having been covered by plenty of other songs, though rarely with such intensity. What really makes 'Man Out Of Time' special is the chorus, which although only two lines long radically alters the song's direction. From the opening lines of the first verse I get the impression that the woman and the narrator are on the trail of the man, and have reached the place he hid in (perhaps a cheap hotel room) during his flight from her. This establishes the theme of a quest, which in the chorus becomes a quest for love. All the evil decay of the verses is forgotton as the narrator desperately asks her if she can love 'a man out of time'. This phrase is in itself richly ambiguous: on one level it means having run out of time, having endured so much and not being able to take any more. As on *Get Happy!!* he's at breaking point, and throws his proud posturings overboard in a last ditch attempt to stay afloat. But on another level 'out of time' means just that, outside time. This is Costello's most extreme expression of outsiderdom: to be outside time is a terrifying prospect, the ultimate in being severed from the rest of the world. The narrator seems to fear that he's losing his grasp on reality, and needs the woman's love to prevent him drifting off aimlessly into featureless infinity. As in the coda to 'Beyond Belief' he's had enough of always being on the outside and recognises that love is necessary in order to draw and hold him in.

What makes 'Man Out Of Time' so effective is the contrast between the apparent certainty of the verses in which the failings of the world are castigated, and the self-doubt of the chorus where the narrator longs to enter that world. He's spent so long scorning and despising the world that it's going to be hard to live with it, but he certainly can't live without it.

'Almost Blue' is the album's only song not to be heavily produced. There's just Nieve's delicate piano plus discreet bass and drums behind Costello's vocals, and the result shines out in its simplicity and heartfeltness. I've given the title 'almost-love song' to a handful of earlier pieces, and this description perfectly suits 'Almost Blue'. It features the word 'almost' no fewer than ten times, giving us the impression that the relationship the song describes has come so near to succeeding and yet so far from it.

The couple have been close enough to happiness to be able to recognise it in the distance, but somehow they just haven't been able to reach it, so there's a heartbreaking sense of falling short. The narrator admits to being a 'fool', perhaps because in the past he hasn't taken love seriously enough and only realises its importance now it's too late. So as in 'Man Out Of Time' we feel that he is stretching out for something like a man clinging to a cliff-face seeking a handhold, but with an overpowering sense of doom. 'Almost Blue' seems to suggest that he's not quite going to make it; despite its lack of electronic wizardry the song is one of the most electric on the whole album – you hardly dare to breathe while it's playing for fear of upsetting its perilous balance.

From the simplest to one of the grandest – '. . . and in Every Home', as it is oddly titled, is Costello's first song to feature an orchestra, (bass and drums appear too), arranged by Nieve. In fact the effect is quite unlike the epic scale of 'Man Out Of Time', but is instead almost jokily flamboyant, as is some of the lyric. It's loosely about unemployment, but like 'Ghost Train' before it, it doesn't approach this subject in an openly political way, preferring instead to dwell on the human angle. A shadowy story underlies the song. In the first verse we see a couple at home. She is still in bed (a 'slag heap' because it's so untidy, but also cheekily and maybe sexistly categorising her) because she's got no job to get up for – in the chorus anonymous voices politely but unfeelingly turn the couple down. The story ends with the husband in prison – he's probably turned to crime because of his lack of work – while the wife has affairs with his friends. Essentially then this is a poignant song about the waste of lives and the destruction of a marriage. In the middle it's pointed out that he has become a 'has-been' even though he's probably still quite young: unemployment has ruined his life completely, and while Costello is too subtle an artist to moralise we get the message. Unemployment is a social disaster; still, at least the song provided temporary employment for a fair few instrumentalists.

Side two swings into life with 'The Loved Ones', another song with a baffling complexity of personages and perspectives, taken at an enjoyably hectic pace. The only obvious unity is that it's a collection of bitcheries, apparently spoken by and addressed to a variety of people – there is a narrator, but he speaks in his own voice only occasionally, such as at the end of the first verse. The context in which all these snide remarks are made is also far from clear, but perhaps it's a wedding (as in 'Imperial Bedroom'), sometimes occasions for families to come together and indulge in a bit of insult jousting in a slander session. The title is of course heavily ironic (there seeming to be little love lost here) as must be the coda. Here the narrator repeatedly spells out letter by letter 'PPS I love you'. But even though this is said with superficial sarcasm, after some of the heartfelt cries on the first side we're inclined to think that there's at least a grain of sincerity in it. 'The Loved Ones' is rather irritatingly obscure, but has plenty of good individual lines, and any song that rhymes 'poison' with 'boys and' must have something going for it.

'Human Hands' is that rarest of things, a virtually unambiguous love song from Costello, (though he can't resist going off at tangents in the second and beginning of the third verses). By the time *Imperial Bedroom* was released in July 1982 he'd been making records for over five years, and in all his prolific output not one of his original songs dares to make an unequivocal declaration of love. Such feelings have been implied many times, of course, but previously his narrators have felt the need to hide them behind masks of indifference and disgust, to conceal them in the middle of tortuous mazes of verbiage. It's ironic that when it's at last said aloud and without qualification it comes on his most wordy, polysyllabically discursive album. The simple phrase 'I love you' stands out among the extravagantly elaborate lines all around it like a toothbrush in a palace. But the point is that even people who live in palaces need toothbrushes: oil paintings on the walls and silver cutlery on the tables are all very well, but unless they're accompanied by the basic necessities of life they can hardly be enjoyed. In 'Human Hands' Costello the songwriter finally openly admits this, and at last the move away from cynical outsiderdom is complete.

But if 'Human Hands' is a love song it's by no means an entirely orthodox one. The situation described in the first verse – the lovers are separated, and he longs for her – is entirely familiar from countless other pop songs, but Costello's idiosyncratic lyric puts a new gloss on it. For example, his solitude is emphasised by references to the hostility of the world outside. He has the television on with the sound turned down, so the programme's 'threats and false alarms' are bizarrely silent and alien. As in 'Man Out Of Time' he needs love to protect him from the chaos surrounding him. Unfortunately, though, it seems from the chorus

101

that the course of his love is not running smooth. He keeps saying the wrong things, causing her to doubt his sincerity, which, thinking back to many of Costello's earlier songs, strikes me as a not entirely unreasonable attitude for her to take. Being the recipient of, for example, 'Human Touch' must be to say the least a mixed blessing. But now the narrator is anxious to dispel all doubts, and wants only to submit to her embrace. The stress on *'human* hands' suggests that he recognises that she has her defects but is willing to take her, faults and all. Earlier songs rejoice in finding fault, so this turnaround to unconditional surrender in recognition of an ordinary human need is really rather moving, like Scrooge's conversion at the end of Dickens' *Christmas Carol*.

'Human Hands', then, is a soul-baring song, and 'Kid About It' is the opposite side of the same coin. Having risked utter honesty himself the narrator now begs his partner to do the same. The song begins as a third person narrative, though pleas addressed to 'you' are interjected, but the last verse is in the first person, and this transition from the distant to the intimate mimics his attempts to get closer to her. 'Kid About It' is indeed a song in which he is trying very hard, but as in 'Almost Blue' tragically not quite succeeding. This is most evident in the chorus, where the voice strains up to the very top of its range as he beseeches her not to 'kid about it'. She is evidently not treating their relationship seriously, so there's a streak of the 'Miracle Man' tease in her. The word 'kid', moreover, implies that she is behaving imma-turely, which reinforces the idea that he has had enough of adolescent playing around and wants to settle down to the real thing. I find the desire in 'Kid About It' to leave behind his previous stance of studied indifference and to enter into a genuine commitment completely convincing. The power of the song, as in several others from the album, comes from its sense of yearning. We feel that he really is ready and willing to make any sacrifice to achieve a fulfilled relationship, but that sadly he's not going to succeed.

The two preceding songs long for love, but with 'Little Savage' we're back with the complexities and failures of relationships. In some respects it's another love song – the chorus is, superficially at least, full of gratitude to the narrator's lover, and contains a beautiful image of reconciliation ultimately drawn from the Bible (Isaiah 11:6, to be precise: 'The wolf also shall dwell with the lamb, and the leopard shall lie down with the kid; and the calf and the young lion and the fatling together' – one of Costello's rare literary allusions). But even here there's a disturbing ambiguity: is 'savage' an adjective or a noun? This might sound a purely academic point, but actually it's crucial to the meaning of the song. If it's an adjective then the title means that he is just a little bit savage – perhaps he used to be even more so, but has become civilised since, as Costello's evolving persona has. But if it's a noun then he's a savage who happens to be little. The former interpretation is probably the first one we think of, but as the song progresses the more unpleasant latter reading dawns on us, especially as the vocals dwell on the word 'savage' towards the end in what might be taken to be an ominous way. So if he is warning that he has the potential to behave barbarously even the chorus isn't as positive as it appears at first sight.

It's ironic that the song should rest on a fine point of the interpretation of words, because one of its main themes is that of the inadequacy of language. The couple's problem seems to be that they talk and talk, generate whole balloonfuls of 'hot air', but without really communicating. The proverb 'actions speak louder than words' is quoted, which threatens to seriously devalue Costello's word hoard. In the last verse the narrator despairs of being able to make meaningful contact via language, and resorts to drink (as do the narrators of several middle-period songs). 'Little Savage' questions the efficacy of the whole of Costello's art: his songs rely heavily on their lyrics for their effectiveness, but if words are ineffectual, where does that leave them and him? The song is not only a fairly effective portrait of a difficult relationship, but also a brave piece of self examination.

For the first years of his recording career Costello was so overflowing with ideas for songs that the question of collaborating in writing them probably hardly arose. He was writing almost too many without anyone else's help – if someone else had chipped in too then the land would have been awash with Costello songs. But in recent years he has been involved in several collaborations, the first of them being 'Boy With A Problem'. Most of the lyric is by Chris Difford of Squeeze, but it's so characteristically Costellian in manner and subject that if this information weren't on the sleeve then you'd never guess it. The song follows straight on from 'Little Savage', and depicts a marriage going through a rocky period. The husband-narrator is drinking again, and the couple's relationship has deteriorated to the point where they both commit minor acts of violence against the other. He doesn't want to end the marriage, but as so often before has a sense of things inexorably slipping away from him. But, quite unexpectedly, in the very last line it's suggested that she might be able to forgive him, despite all his boorish behaviour, so in the end 'Boy With A Problem' is one of the album's most hopeful songs.

I like 'Pidgin English' a lot, but trying to explain why is infuriatingly difficult. It's one of the most fiendishly convoluted songs, and despite puzzling over it for a long time I find myself unable to say with much confidence what it's about. So you're advised to take my comments with an even larger pinch of salt than you're no doubt by now accustomed to sprinkle over them. Language appears to be a theme once more, 'pidgin English' perhaps referring to the semi-literate collection of clichés that passes for communication between some people. They hardly seem to be aware that their conversations consist entirely of banalities – they wouldn't recognise a cliché if you handed them one on a platitude. In part the song is an attack on such people, and the limited scope of their lives. The couple in the first verse, and especially the feckless man, are subjected to the narrator's scorn, but it's uncertain if either of them are to be identified with the 'you' addressed in the rest of the song. 'You' probably means us, the listeners, so we are being directly admonished in the chorus. Here we're told and asked 'there are ten commandments of love, when will you realise?' This might imply that we often disregard the unwritten rules of behaviour in our relationships and that we need to watch our step in case we become like the couple in the previous song. The admonishment is sad rather than angry, however – the narrator has perhaps ruined his own life in this way and can't stand seeing other people behave so carelessly. The last verse cautions us to use whatever powers of communication we have to start making amends before it's too late.

The coda's 'PS I love you' is not as obviously ironic as that of 'The Loved Ones', but nevertheless is hard to take entirely seriously. Who's it addressed to, for one thing? Us, still? Such philanthropy seems unlikely. The woman in the first verse? The rest of the song doesn't support this. It could be simply an example of the sort of thing we ought to be saying, if anything can be said to be simple in this Sphinx-like, baffling but irresistible song.

Thankfully we're on safer ground in 'You Little Fool', which is relatively straightforward but wonderfully realised. It's another song with a story, concerning a teenage girl and her desire to enter the adult world, to put on 'big sister's clothes', as *Trust* has it. Her father still treats her like a little girl, spoiling her and refusing to acknowledge that she has a life and mind of her own; her mother on the other hand is blasé about her daughter's burgeoning sexuality and doles out contraceptives with alacrity. The song implies that neither of these attitudes is responsible or constructive, for she falls for the oily charms of a bar-room Lothario, failing to see through his falsity. The word 'imitation' is frequently reiterated, especially in the last verse which is set in a bar that is attempting to be up-market, probably serving pina coladas and prawn cocktail flavour crisps. Fakery and deception is a constant theme of Costello's songs, often inspiring him to flights of rage, but in the chorus there's only concerned sorrow as she's rebuked for being a 'little fool'. *Imperial Bedroom* is full of dejection over the messes people make of their lives and nowhere is this more agonisingly but briskly expressed than in 'You Little Fool'.

The album concludes, appropriately after so much anguish, with another song of personal vulnerability, 'Town Cryer' (as the sleeve insists on misspelling it). This presents a familiar persona, the injured innocent, though he's certainly come a long way since the days of, say, 'I'm Not Angry' when such open admissions of being hurt would be unthinkable. The narrator now feels no shame in describing himself as a 'town crier', indeed, he is anxious to make his tears public. The usual meaning of the phrase 'town crier' is also relevant, however, as the function of such people is to alert the world to significant events; all Costello's records take upon themselves the task of telling us what's going on, only the bell he rings to attract attention is usually an alarm bell.

The tone of the song is introspective, the major seventh chord (not often used by Costello) in the introduction and first line adding a bitter-sweet edge. As in 'Human Hands' he fears having his sincerity doubted, and asks us to reassure ourselves by examining his face, and it's true that in Costello's photograph on the sleeve, where he appears distinctly melancholy despite the jolly straw boater, he looks us squarely in the eye. So we are inclined to take the song (literally) at face value, and accept it as a directly personal confession.

His resolve to be happy and outward-looking carries no conviction; it is produced as a kind of magic charm that will solve all his problems, but with no real faith in its efficacy. Even his description of the carefree youths he'd like to emulate makes them sound far from angst-free. They use their 'trembling lip[s]' to seduce women and charm the world, a phrase firstly suggesting Presley-like sexily disdainful pouts and grimaces, but also making it sound as if they're about to burst into tears themselves. It seems as if we are all doomed to live in a vale of misery; we can either be aloof outsiders, a policy which might work for a while but becomes intolerably lonely, or enter the teeming stage of life, which is even more demanding and complex. The song (and the album) concludes that 'love and unhappiness go arm in arm', which is fatalistic even by Costello's gloomy standards. If *Imperial Bedroom* is a quest for some satisfaction to replace the dissatisfaction so prominently expressed on the earlier albums, then it ends not much further on than from where it started. A few bruises and scratches have been collected along the way, but the journey has been in some ways a vain one. Happiness has not been achieved, yet we have the impression that the journey has been an enriching experience, and that Costello – and the listener – are the wiser and the better for it. The long fade out (with rather too schmaltzy strings, but fine piano and brass) lets such thoughts run through our mind before our record player's stylus makes its own inevitable journey back to the place where it started.

Trust is perhaps Costello's least personal album; *Imperial Bedroom* is possibly at the other end of the same scale. I make this judgment both because of the confessional nature of many of the songs, and because of the relative paucity of references to political issues. Every other album contains pieces that can broadly be classified as personal and those that I've chosen to call public, but *Imperial Bedroom* is very heavily biased towards the former. There are no songs that can be unconditionally classified as public; 'Man Out Of Time' has some bearing on the theme of the corruption of power, but its crux is clearly the narrator's search for emotional salvation; '. . . and in Every Home' has the best claim to be included in this category, but unemployment is not presented in an overtly political way, the song focuses instead on its effects on individuals; 'Pidgin English' is partly about language, but again this public theme is given very personal expression. Naturally some other songs contain the odd line here and there (a few of them very odd) which reminds us that there are events and issues outside our ordinary everyday ones, but basically the album is about the emotions, and more specifically the emotional problems, of individuals.

The literal self-effacement evident on about half of *Trust*'s songs has gone, and we're back with a heavy emphasis on first person narrators directly involved in the song's circumstances. Only one is entirely in the third person ('The Long Honeymoon'), though another two are mostly so ('... and in Every Home' and 'You Little Fool'). The remaining dozen are as directly personal and immediate as those on *Get Happy!!*; *Imperial Bedroom* certainly gives the impression of coming straight from the heart.

The coda of 'Beyond Belief' seems to imply that this determination to become involved is a deliberate policy. A brief recap might be useful here: *My Aim Is True, This Year's Model* and *Armed Forces* (especially the first two) are quite consciously written from the point of view of an outsider. The narrators of the songs are for the most part extremely cynical about relationships and consequently do their best not to get involved with women, or if they do get involved take every opportunity to announce their supposed indifference. This is a pose, of course, as the sub-text of song after song reveals, but nevertheless they try to keep their distance; the perfect image of this is the front of *This Year's Model* with Costello safe behind his camera. *Get Happy!!* is quite different: the narrators now no longer hang back on the sidelines but plunge straight in, very nearly drowning themselves in the process. It's almost too much to cope with, and after this traumatic experience they again become observers rather than participants, hence the high proportion of *Trust* songs without narrators. Although they remain deeply cynical about relationships the experience has taught them the prime importance of love, and purged them of much of their anger and disgust. In one or two songs they even show a tentative desire to get involved with women once again.

This brings us up to *Imperial Bedroom*. To continue my earlier metaphor, having learnt from their previous disaster in *Get Happy!!* the narrators' approach is this time not so reckless, and instead of diving in head first they immerse themselves step by step, aware of the dangers but determined to face them and overcome them. Every single song on the album is about relationships, and while there are still a few hefty chunks of cynicism (witness 'The Loved Ones') in general the narrators no longer want to smash everything that goes wrong like children throwing toys that won't work against the wall. Instead they tend to try to effect repairs by nursing and cosseting, most obviously in 'Human Hands' and 'Kid About It'. Reprisal has been prominent on the earlier albums, but now a desire for reconciliation takes its place. Consequently *Imperial Bedroom* is, with the possible exception of *King Of America*, Costello's most positive and constructive album.

Unfortunately, this doesn't mean that it's any happier than any of the others. 'Love and unhappiness go arm in arm' could easily stand as its epigraph. For all the longing there is not one unambiguously fulfilled song, and most of them are profoundly miserable. To some extent women get the blame for this, a return to the attitude of the first albums. Even 'Human Hands', probably Costello's nearest approach to a happy love song so far, implies that his lover has to be constantly appeased. But men (including the narrators themselves) get just as much, if not more, criticism, and more importantly the album is only marginally concerned with apportioning blame in order to make accusations. It continues *Trust*'s trend towards understanding and compassion rather than simply exploding with rage and disgust. There are even a few quasi-religious touches, such as leanings towards forgiveness, the 'ten commandments of love', and the Biblical allusion in 'Little Savage'. I've already used some theological terms in trying to capture *Imperial Bedroom*'s individual flavour, not because I want to suggest that there are any signs of Costello embracing Christianity or any other religion, but because of the album's combination of humility and a quest for inner calm. (It's interesting to note that a 1982 single, a cover of Smokey Robinson's 'From Head to Toe', is also an expression of self-abasement, albeit presented in a much more conventional pop format.) The objection often raised about Costello's songs – that they are violent and vindictive, the product of a twisted sensitivity – is only intermittently valid here. More often *Imperial Bedroom* has a generosity of spirit and a refreshing openness.

As if immediately repenting of this, however, it covers its tracks by indulging in a bout of bewildering complexity. This applies both to the production of the music, as I've already discussed, and to the lyrics. For the first time they are frankly printed on the inner sleeve, a gesture indicative of a desire not to be misheard, and possibly not to be misunderstood either. But to counter this the lyrics are printed in such a way as to make reading them as hard as possible – no punctuation, no breaks between lines or between songs. This seems like a slightly shame-faced way to disguise their revealing nature. Furthermore, although the lyrics are revealing in that they seem to tell us, when read closely, a lot about Costello's frame of mind, they are even more elaborate and occasionally elusive than before. Costello has always delighted in using his articulacy, but on *Imperial Bedroom* this reaches new peaks. He's not afraid to say things simply when necessary, as in 'Human Hands', but more often the 'verbal gymnastics' are dazzling. We cannot fail to be impressed by the dexterity of the word-play – every song contains some deft reworkings of clichés, or puns at once witty and revealing, or turns of phrase that go straight to the heart of the matter. The album's use of metaphors is a *tour de force*; it would have been easy to write a chapter of this length devoted only to expounding them. This baroque complexity of language does have its drawbacks, however – one or two of the songs and many lines seem to me to be virtually impenetrable. This is by no means confined to *Imperial Bedroom*, but sometimes I get the impression that elaborate phrases are used not for communication but for display.

One aspect of the album's complexity we can wholeheartedly welcome is its multiplicity of melodies. It's arguably Costello's most tuneful album. All but three of the songs have a middle as well as verses and chorus, (the middles of 'The Long Honeymoon' and 'Pidgin English' are instrumental), and this is indicative of the free flow of melodic ideas. They spring up everywhere, fresh and ebullient, as if there's simply no end to Costello's melodic invention. Especially attractive are the tunes of the ballad-like songs, such as 'The Long Honeymoon' and 'Town Cryer', but the faster numbers like '. . . and in Every Home' and 'Human Hands' are extremely singable too. Several of them deserve to become pop standards on the strength of their music alone, and there aren't too many songs by Costello you can say that about. All in all *Imperial Bedroom*, coming as it does after *Get Happy!!* and *Trust*, is a fitting climax to a trilogy of unquestionable quality.

The album has a title track which for some inscrutable reason was not included on it. The phrase 'Imperial Bedroom', suggesting as Costello remarked a 'combination of splendour and sleaze', but also, like 'Emotional Fascism', implying that personal behaviour is a mirror for political events and vice versa, is a resonant one. So it's not surprising that he couldn't resist using it as a song title. The result was first released on the B-side of the twelve-inch version of 'Man Out Of Time'. 'Imperial Bedroom' is a delightfully wry waltz, with a stronger narrative element than usual. It tells the story of a bride who sleeps with her husband-to-be's best man in the honeymoon hotel. Human weaknesses are viewed with tolerance and even amusement; there's none of the anguish to be found on the album. It's a deceptively slight song – the surface is almost vapid, but this hides the depth of feeling, the sorrow at the idiotic things people do. It's as good as most of the songs on the album.

Two songs appeared on the B-side of 'You Little Fool': 'Big Sister', which was mentioned in the previous chapter, and 'Stamping Ground', one of my least favourites. It's about the empty life of a woman who spends most of her life in a bar. It conveys the incestuousness and sterility of the cliques of convenience who gather in such places; solitude is anathema to them, every second has to be occupied by some facile activity to prevent the possibility of a thought entering their minds.

Costello's last release of 1982 was a single called 'Party Party'. It was written for a film of the same name, which promptly sank without trace, all hands going down with it. Costello does not rate this song highly, and while agreeing that it's no masterpiece I rather like it. It quite neatly sums up the way in which people always expect parties to be fun but often end up being made all the more miserable by them. It's also something of a signpost for things to come, for it features gutsy, raucous rhythm'n'blues brass for the first time (the orchestral brass of *Imperial Bedroom* is not the same thing at all). This presages the opening notes of the next album in which the TKO Horns breezily announce themselves.

8

'Punch The Clock'

Imperial Bedroom is a magnificent album, whatever minor reservations one might have about it. Yet Costello evidently was not entirely happy with it: it reached a respectable though not stunning number six in the UK album chart but didn't stay long, received mixed reviews and, what's more, both the singles taken from it failed to reach the top fifty. The album hardly received the artistic and commercial acclaim it merited, but, as Costello's songs are so fond of explaining, there's no justice in the world. *Imperial Bedroom* had been a not entirely successful change of direction; what was needed was another change of direction, to get closer to the promised land of perfection beyond the horizon.

One result of this change was a different approach to sleeve design. That of *Imperial Bedroom* is positively eccentric, with its 'Snakecharmer and Reclining Octopus' painting, allegedly dating from 1942. It's certainly different, but has little if any relevance to the album's contents and can hardly have seduced many people into buying it. The sleeve of *Punch The Clock* is very different – it's far more conventional than those of any other Costello album. The front features what's virtually a pin-up picture; Costello looks like a man out of *Time* magazine complete with fashionably tousled hair and his latest entry in the novelty hat competition (later won hands down by *King Of America*'s crown). On the back he and the band gaze moodily (or possibly blankly) into the distance. Rock performers have featured in identical poses on countless other albums. The sleeve of *Punch The Clock* is clearly an attempt to reassure the record-buying public that what they'll find inside won't be too outlandish.

More importantly, for *Punch The Clock* Costello again changed his producer, for the third album running. The production of

Imperial Bedroom had been one of its questionable aspects, and so Clive Langer and Alan Winstanley appear on the scene. Their previous commercial successes, with Madness for example, must have suggested that if anyone could give Costello's next record some chart clout, then they could. (Langer had also written the exquisite music for 'Shipbuilding', but I'll deal with that later.) Consequently *Punch The Clock* is the most persuasive piece of pop music since *Armed Forces*.

Also crucial to the album's direction is the presence of the TKO Horns, an ensemble specially assembled for the occasion. The combination of trumpet, trombone and alto and tenor saxes, although appearing on only five of the thirteen tracks, adds a new dimension of sound. Although the brass isn't as throatily soulful as I'd have liked (I'd have preferred it to be more brash and rough as it is on those great sixties soul records, Sam and Dave's 'Hold On, I'm Coming', for example), it helps the album live up to its title by being punchy. Furthermore, four tracks feature Afrodiziak, a female vocal duo, who also expand the musical possibilities. The album still often features an electronically rallied choir of Costellos, but now he doesn't have to harmonise with himself all the time. The sleeve could have credited the record with some justification to the Elvis Costello Big Band.

The album blasts off with the TKO Horns doing their utmost to send it into orbit. The brass riff to 'Let Them All Talk' is tremendously vigorous, its falling phrases generating enough power to light a small town. The riff is basically in D minor, and some of the song's excitement comes from the tension between this and the rest of the song, which is basically in D major. This is exactly the same modulation that helps make 'No Dancing' from the first album so piquant, and the effect is similar here. The Fs and Cs are sometimes sharp but sometimes natural, and this ambiguity enlivens the music. Listening as the harmonies mesh and seem to be about to clash, but always just succeed in resolving themselves, puts you on the edge of your seat.

Which is just as well, really, as the lyric is not very substantial and wouldn't hold the attention were it not for the exhilaration of the music. The words are very abstract, unlike most of Costello's other songs, which are monologues spoken from a specific situation. The theme of time has not been prominent on the two previous albums, but 'Let Them All Talk' is fundamentally a stern reminder that time passes and is irrecoverable. This is clear in the middle and parts of the last verse, but exactly how it relates to the rest of the song I'm not sure. I can't see the reason behind the apparent dig at Talking Heads' 'Psycho Killer'. Despite the first line's schoolmasterish injunction to pay attention, I'm not much the wiser by the end.

'Everyday I Write The Book' is a song of unrequited love for a familiarly siren-like woman. It's also Costello's most immediately catchy number for some time, credit for this going partly to Langer and Winstanley. I heard Costello perform this song on the 1982 tour, when it was taken at insipid pace and sounded droopily maudlin. But the producers rejuvenated it, and the 1983 version strikes just the right balance between amused self mockery and genuine anguish. Nieve's tinkling keyboards create infectious counter-rhythms, Afrodiziak chime in on the choruses, and all in all it's a delicious song. (The video, featuring Prince and Princess of Wales lookalikes getting on each other's nerves in a small flat was fun too, albeit without much to do with the lyric.)

It uses thematic punning (the first time this technique has been extensively used since *Get Happy!!*) drawn from writing, and wryly acknowledges the Mills and Boon nature of the affair. But here there's no happy ending, and the narrator is left with only his pen and paper for comfort. This is all done almost jokily, but there's also an edge of genuine pain. What's more, the song can be taken as a confession that he writes the 'book' as a substitute for having her; if you like you can extend this idea so that all his feelings of dissatisfaction, frustration and yearning are transmuted into art. Perhaps this explains why there are very few happy songs by Costello.

As if to immediately confound this theory the next song turns out to be a happy one. It's the last thing you'd expect from the author of 'Shot With His Own Gun', but 'The Greatest Thing' is a paean to marriage. It features a woman who, almost uniquely in Costello's songs, is the subject of apparently unambiguous and unstinting praise. This is the positive side of the theme of women-as-demi-goddesses: all the awe and adoration, but none of the fear. To be married to such a wonderful creature is 'the greatest thing'; it's even suggested that such a marriage is an escape from the tyranny of time. This is where the album's title, *Punch The Clock*, comes in. At first this phrase suggests clocking in for work at the factory in the morning (as in 'Let Them All Talk'), but here it suggests smashing and stopping time. Love as a kind of access to immortality is admittedly rather a far-fetched idea (though it does crop up in literature occasionally – see Shakespeare's first seventeen sonnets, for example), but as a metaphor for the liberation from humdrum day-to-day concerns and worries that ecstatic love can bring it's not bad.

The song is careful to point out that by no means all marriages are like this. Like 'Big Sister's Clothes' it berates those who marry without seriously thinking about the consequences, using plenty of snappy rhyming and barbed wit in doing so. But despite this the song is fundamentally an exuberant shout of joy. This is most evident in the first entry of the brass: up to this point the song has been in the unusual key of A flat major, but as the horns surge forward there's an astonishing modulation to E major. Suddenly the flats bloom into sharps, and the music is reborn, and life-giving. 'The Greatest Thing' is the most conservative of all Costello's songs in the attitudes it expresses, but musically it's invigorating.

The first three songs get the album off to a promising start, but unfortunately the next two dissipate the momentum. The first of these, 'The Element Within Her', is another song about a demigoddess. The chorus, with its references to precious stones, almost literally turns her into an idol. Not that he's idolising her as that word is usually used – he's too well aware of her haughtiness and disdain. The song also features a charming but witless man, but how he fits in we aren't told. In fact much of the song is embarrassingly weak, especially the last two verses. Costello just doesn't seem to have had his heart in this; how else can you account for one of rock's greatest lyricists singing 'la la la' like an inane Eurovision Song Contest hopeful?

'Love Went Mad' is not quite as bad, but it still sounds like it could have been tossed off in a few minutes, and no one would have been much the poorer had it then been tossed away. It's a curious hybrid – the chorus from an anguished unrequited love song, the verses from a song of denunciation. The former laments the way in which all the narrator's relationships self-destruct, and brusquely appeals for sympathy, but in such a manner that we're more likely to be irritated by its demands. The latter attempt to be pungent and witty but fail. Well, it's comforting to know that even Costello doesn't always find it easy.

'Shipbuilding' was first released as a single by Robert Wyatt in 1982. With music by Clive Langer and lyrics by Costello, it was a response to the Falklands War, then only recently ended. You might have expected Costello to be stung into a virulently angry attack on the government's bellicose reply to the Argentinians' invasion – after all, *Armed Forces* is devoted to denouncing militarism, and the whole affair should arguably have been handled with diplomacy, not brute force. But, perhaps in response to the beautifully plaintive tune, what he came up with is sadly ruminative rather than angry.

It's sung in the persona of an unemployed shipyard worker at the beginning of the war, and delicately balances his entirely understandable desire for the yards to open again, so he can earn some money, with dismay at what the ships he'll help make will do. The opening lines are touchingly human, as he turns over in his mind the things he'll be able to afford to buy for his family if work becomes available. The chorus shows the ripples of excitement running around the town with the rumours that the yards are going to start taking on workers. So far the song is a sympathetic portrait of a depressed port, a victim of the unemployment plague of the seventies and eighties. There are no other jobs available to the men laid off by the yards; shipbuilding is their way of life and they've been exiled from it.

Yet Costello quietly reminds us that in this case the ships are going to be built (or refitted) for purposes which will include killing people in a possibly unjust cause. This point certainly isn't stridently over-emphasised, but is made subtly by, for example, alluding to the expectations of August 1914 that the First World War would 'all be over by Christmas', reminding us of the millions of deaths that eventually resulted. Similarly many people embarked on the Falklands War full of jingoism and hopes of glory, forgetting the inevitable suffering and loss of life it would bring. Lives are being misused, people are fighting, killing and being killed rather than searching for happiness and fulfillment – 'diving for pearls' in Costello's magical phrase.

The regret at the human waste is evocatively echoed by Langer's music – especially effective are the flattened Es in the chorus, which create a sense of dignified mourning. The exquisitely elegaic trumpet solo, played by jazz musician Chet Baker (who tragically died in 1988 after falling from an Amsterdam hotel window), is near-perfect, and makes even the best rock musicians sound hamfisted and unimaginative.

'Shipbuilding' is undoubtedly a great song, but I'm afraid I have my reservations about this particular performance of it. The keyboard power-chords which introduce it are too aggressive for a quietly reflective song, and why does Costello pause before and spit out the word 'children'? Also the end is over-demonstrative. It sounds very much as if all involved in recording it were conscious of competing with Wyatt's superb version, and tried to go one better by making their version more elaborate. In my opinion this was a misjudgment, and while I'll continue to listen to *Punch The Clock*'s interpretation of the song for the sake of Baker's solo, in every other respect I prefer the original.

Side two begins brazenly with 'TKO (Boxing Day)'. As its title suggests it reintroduces the TKO Horns, who are on thunderously good form and carry the song along at a blistering pace. Perhaps the hope is that we won't listen to the words, for the lyric is distasteful in the extreme. It uses thematic punning drawn from boxing, and although this is done with some measure of skill I only wish that some of this skill had been lavished on making the song a bit more humane. Its subject is a relationship in which the man (the narrator) brutalises his partner, and apparently relishes every minute of it. He spends the first verse telling her she can't escape, in the second he revels in violence and in the third berates her for not looking attractive when he happens to feel randy. All these are accompanied by physical threats – the chorus consists simply of the letters 'TKO' (Technical Knock-Out). Several Costello songs involve violence against women, but generally with some kind of distancing irony to signal that the violence is not approved of. But there's absolutely no sign in 'TKO' that this is the case. Consequently it reads like a wife-beater's manifesto. It's a nasty song, as subtle as a fist in the face. I've been trying to think of some kind of excuse for it, but I can't.

'Charm School', like several of the songs on side one, is fairly abstract and vague, but seems to be set in clubland, which in turn is perhaps a metaphor for life in general. Its main theme is the difficulty of living a happy life, which is expressed by describing an unsatisfactory relationship. The implication is that the only way to get on in the world is to be coldly ruthless, because if you don't tread on the other person they'll tread on you. Thus in the middle we hear how hopes are crushed, though the narrator longs to find love (as on *Imperial Bedroom*). The mental image 'Charm School' creates for me is of a sleazy subterranean bar populated by various shady characters, all smiling but trying to get the better of their fellows by hook or by crook, trying to get a nose ahead in the rat race. Like a few other *Punch The Clock* songs this could have done with a bit of polishing, but at least does seem to have some real feeling behind it. I like too the piano and bass riffs, the awkward rising and falling intervals of which suit the uncertainty and unease of the lyric.

'The Invisible Man' is one of the album's most successful songs, deftly and wittily dealing with a serious subject, the dehumanisation of modern life. The first line is crammed with teasing meaning. The narrator was 'committed to life', which can be taken in two ways. Firstly it suggests that he was determined to get the most out of life, but it has echoes of being sentenced to life imprisonment. So already this line is double-edged, suggesting naive enthusiasm being ruthlessly quashed. The line continues, adding that he then 'commuted to the outskirts'. The pun on 'commuted' (travelled to work/had his sentence lightened) suggests that he has been got out of the way by being pushed out to the edge of life where he's ignored and forgotten. This is a marvellously concise expression of the manner in which ordinary people are shoved around by the authorities; the rest of the verse shows how they are dissuaded from complaining about their treatment by being given television as a placebo, as children are given lollipops to suck.

The second verse concerns another branch of the media, the cinema. Films exaggerate emotions to such an extent that viewers become discontented with their own lives, instead longing vainly for the make-believe world on the screen. The chorus pursues this theme, asking bewilderedly how real love can be found in an increasingly artificial life. This could sound simply mawkish, but is done with a lightness of touch that saves it from sentimentality. Because of the falsity and lack of humanity all around him the narrator wants to escape, but he can't: he's like the 'invisible man' because everyone just discounts him, he's doomed once again to act out the role of the outsider.

The middles of Costello's songs usually add a new dimension, but here the middle is the weakest part, not telling us anything we couldn't deduce from the rest. The last verse, however, is a real development. In it the narrator's feeling of alienation causes him to have a nightmare vision of a totalitarian world, in which the authorities doctor factual records and use the media to quell dissent by appealing to the baser instincts of the crowd. As in

117

several earlier songs, this looks as if it were inspired by *Nineteen Eighty-Four* – as the album was released in 1983, the year of the Thatcher government's second general election victory, the sense of foreboding is obvious.

The deceptively playful tone is sealed in the coda, which briefly quotes the Beatles' 'You Won't See Me', but nevertheless this is an essentially serious song. The disquiet felt at some repressive tendencies in society, and the fear of what will happen to misfits in such circumstances, are very real.

The next song, 'Mouth Almighty', is also an expression of alienation, but is presented in a purely personal way. It's a confession that the narrator has the habit of saying the wrong thing, upsetting and angering his partner. As an admission of culpability it's similar to some of the *Imperial Bedroom* songs, especially 'Human Hands', but despite this promising pedigree it's surely one of Costello's weakest. The imagery of the first verse could have come from any maudlin love song with pretensions to being poetry, and the whole thing reeks of adolescent self-pity. Usually we're on the side of Costello's outsider persona, but I can't feel anything for him in this case except irritation.

Costello's albums contain plenty of warnings about the way in which big business allegedly mistreats small people, from 'Welcome to the Working Week' through 'Senior Service' to 'Opportunity'. 'King of Thieves' belongs with these; some of its lines are the most direct statements on this theme to be found in any of his songs, although many of the other lines are obscure. It's true that it's not certain that the 'King of Thieves' is some kind of businessman, but all the references to offices, secretaries, typewriters and so on certainly create this impression. In the chorus he and his company are accused of pursuing someone relentlessly and of having absolutely no qualms about how they treat them when they're caught. As the last line says, it would take superhuman courage to stand up to them. Their ruthless pursuit of power is nowhere more clearly shown than in the line 'The moguls want a human sacrifice'. This is hyperbolical, but expresses their complete lack of moral scruples, and is made all the more shocking because the girl they presumably intend to sacrifice appears in the song, thus bringing home to us the human cost of their policies. They won't literally sacrifice her on an altar dedicated to the deity Profit, but her life will nevertheless be ruined by them.

A vein of paranoia runs through the song, as the narrator seems to fear that these unscrupulous people are on his trail too. In the middle he threatens to expose them, but fear gets the better of him and in the last verse he enters their office and joins them, even though he's aware that by doing so he's colluding with their evil schemes. 'King of Thieves', like 'The Invisible Man', is full of foreboding. If the king is now being crowned then this is only the beginning of his reign, and he could go on to make Ivan the Terrible pale by comparison. The song is a dreadful warning along similar lines to 'Night Rally', foreseeing a world ruled by bureaucracies and unelected despots.

Foreboding and fear are even more prominent in 'Pills And Soap'. This was originally released as a single, under the pseudonym The Imposter, just a month before the 1983 general election. The timing was no coincidence – originally the plan was to delete the record on the day of the election in a gesture of defiance, but when it showed signs of being a hit this plan was quietly dropped (it reached number sixteen). This was perhaps Costello's most openly political period; I can remember seeing him on a television chat show of some description at about this time, and hearing him tell the audience in no uncertain terms that they needed their heads examining if they voted Conservative. And in a *Time Out* interview just a month or so after the election he mentioned his support for the Labour Party and commented that, 'If anyone voted for the Tories, well, it serves them right to suffer.' His broadly left-wing sympathies have been obvious since his very first release, 'Less Than Zero', but it's interesting to see that he's prepared to make such specific comments in public.

'Pills And Soap' isn't specifically anti-Tory, (still less specifically pro-Labour), but it does paint a horrifying picture of the cut-throat free-market economy the Conservatives are trying to create. The first and last verses lay in to that old adversary, the media, being particularly scathing about the insensitivity of interviewing people in a state of shock, and the tabloids' attempts to 'cancel any crisis', perhaps remembering the *Sun*'s infamous facile coverage of the Falklands War. The chorus, alluding to the rumours that circulated in the First World War that the Germans boiled dead bodies to make soap, is a macabre Dante-like vision of ruthless and gruesome exploitation of the helpless. I find it hard to listen to 'Pills And Soap' – it's one of Costello's bitterest and most vehement songs, and the effect is, frankly, terrifying. The unrelenting drumbeat that runs through it sounds like a march to the death camps, and the crashing piano chords fall like doom. The song lacks the subtlety, the diplomatic persuasiveness, of most of his other political statements (compare it with 'Shipbuilding', for example) but compensates for this with its sheer unmistakable anger.

I don't think even Costello would want an album to end on such a depressing note, so *Punch The Clock* concludes with 'The World And His Wife', a fairly light-heartedly cynical song about family life. The jaunty brass riff enlivens the tale of a family reunion which begins cheerfully but gradually disintegrates. Sexual attraction intervenes to disrupt the initially well-managed gathering; everyone drinks too much; it comes out that the mother has run away with another man. By the end the reunion is anything but united as all the old resentments and rivalries bubble up, and the last verse ends in literal disharmony with a drunken sing-song 'in different keys'. Thus the album concludes by demolishing another tenet of traditional right-wing faith, the sanctity of the family.

One of the minor disappointments of *Imperial Bedroom* is that it makes very little attempt to get to grips with political issues, but *Punch The Clock* does its best to rectify this. Four songs deal with political (or at least public) subjects: 'Shipbuilding', 'The Invisible Man', 'King of Thieves' and 'Pills And Soap'. In addition several other songs, such as 'Charm School', throw some light on the workings of the world at large without necessarily using this as their main theme. 'Shipbuilding' stands alone here as it makes no attempt to blame or even identify the guilty parties. Only a slightly strained allusion to the Task Force alerts us to the song's subject, the Falklands. What little anger there is in the song is subdued, and consequently it will appeal to a wide range of people of various political persuasions, since everyone can appreciate the human tragedy of the war. 'Pills And Soap', on the other hand, will offend a lot of people, and is no doubt intended to. Its blatant mockery of the aristocracy and jingoistic nationalism is guaranteed to cause much disgust in Tunbridge Wells and many calls for the return of flogging in the correspondence columns of the *Daily Telegraph*. The other two political songs fall somewhere between these two in their approach, 'King of Thieves' veering slightly towards 'Shipbuilding' and 'The Invisible Man' towards 'Pills And Soap'. But despite their varying approaches the theme of fear of a totalitarian future is similar, and *Punch The Clock* is Costello's most sustained and powerful political statement since *Armed Forces*.

The political songs apart I find the album slightly disappointing. It's true that it's quite enjoyable to listen to, for all the reasons that I have discussed at the start of this chapter, and that it contains some good songs. But too many of them are just not up to the standard we expect from Costello. I'd mark out four that are especially weak: 'The Element Within Her', 'Love Went Mad', 'TKO' and 'Mouth Almighty'. Furthermore, even most of the good songs lack intensity and immediacy. Some of the lyrics are too abstract and uninvolving, while some of the attempted verbal gymnastics fall flat on their face. It's revealing that, after the wealth of beautiful tunes of *Imperial Bedroom*, the only melody that really stands out here is 'Shipbuilding', which Costello didn't write. It seems that Costello's apparently effortless ease in writing songs is beginning to desert him, and throughout the album there's the sense of struggling to achieve effects which previously had been brought off with almost arrogant ease. I don't want to be too harsh on the album, however. Costello had set himself the highest possible standards, and it's only when measured against these that the album is a relative anticlimax. Had it been released under the name of any other artist, we should recognise it for what it really is, a varied, provocative and punchy collection of well-above-average songs.

It's certainly true that many of the songs sound good live, in which context the listener can't so easily stop to think about and maybe find fault with their details, but is simply carried along by their impetus. On the 1983 tour Costello and the Attractions were augmented by both the TKO Horns and Afrodiziak, and consequently the shows were exhilarating experiences. They've been compared to the soul revues of the sixties, and this description captures their passion and drive. Some earlier songs had horn parts written in, and the results were sometimes revelatory. The arrangement of 'King Horse', for example, made you wish that a brass section had been included on *Get Happy!!*, and that of 'Watching the Detectives' swung the song along with demented fury. It's a great pity that Costello hasn't used a brass section on any other albums (yet) – the TKO Horns' only other recorded appearance is on a tedious song by Yoko Ono, 'Walking On Thin Ice' (included on *Out Of Our Idiot*).

Two other songs surfaced as B-sides in 1983, both much superior to some of the material that appeared on the album. 'Everyday I Write The Book' was accompanied by 'Heathen Town', an appendix to the album's political songs. It describes a godforsaken world and the narrator's fears that he will be sucked in or under, rather like 'King of Thieves'. On the other side of 'Let Them All Talk' was 'The Flirting Kind', a reflectively tuneful study of a coquette, but viewing her with sympathy rather than disgust. Even if his supremacy in the album field took a bit of a battering, Costello remained undisputed king of the B-side.

9

'Goodbye Cruel World'

If the sleeve of *Punch The Clock*, with its orthodoxly handsome photograph of Costello, signalled an attempt to move into the mainstream of rock and to achieve greater commercial acceptability, then that of 1984's *Goodbye Cruel World* was a further step in the same direction. Instead of portraying Costello and the Attractions in the traditional pop star mould, however, the sleeve is playfully enigmatic, intended to tease and intrigue onlookers in order to encourage them to buy the record in the hope of satisfying their aroused curiosity. The photograph on the front, with its brilliant blue background and artfully posed figures (including a robotic Costello), is certainly eye-catching and cryptic. The cliff, the two trees, the all black or all white clothes, the fencer, appear to possess elusive gnomic significance. The portraits on the back are also rather self-consciously smart. Pete Thomas appears as a transparent, spectral form; Bruce Thomas is seen from the back and is covered by a grid of red and blue lines; there's the unusual spectacle of a spectacleless Costello, and only half his face at that; Nieve's presence is indicated only by a fencer's visor on a rather nasty flowery wallpaper background. Brian Griffin's photography is certainly imaginative and, in its way, successful, but I have to say that I find the sleeve a bit too slick, too concerned with mannered, stagy gestures. This wouldn't matter much if it didn't reflect the music so accurately. In my opinion the songs, like the sleeve, lack depth, though there's enough happening on the surface to stimulate interest, even if expectations thus aroused are never entirely fulfilled.

This is at once apparent in the opening song, 'The Only Flame in Town'. The implicit story is far from new: the narrator has been separated from his lover, who now has a new boyfriend, but the narrator attempts to convince himself, unsuccessfully, that he is unconcerned by this. Similar scenarios have been a part of Costello's method since 'I'm Not Angry' on his first album, and by now the formula is becoming overworked. He tries to spark the song into life by using thematic puns drawn from fire, but no one could claim this as one of Costello's best lyrics.

Few, if any, of Costello's songs are entirely without merit, however, and there are several signs of a nimble intelligence at work. Near the beginning, when the situation is still being established, he states that 'when we're alone we never quarrel', which to begin with the listener takes to mean they don't quarrel when they're alone together, thus indicating a harmonious relationship. The next line, though, laconically adds 'I'm miles away', and we realise that they are not together but separate, and that's the reason they don't quarrel. You have to admire such adept manipulation of the listener's expectations, even when they are almost a matter of routine.

And in the last verse the line 'Even an inferno can cool down to an ember' has a profound haiku-like feel to it. So even such a run-of-the-mill song, unlikely as it is to set the world alight, has its moments.

Musically, 'The Only Flame in Town' is one of the album's glossiest songs. Gary Barnacle's saxes are much in evidence, Daryl Hall's backing vocals add a nice cutting edge and Nieve inserts an irrelevant (and irreverent) quotation from Bach's 'Jesu, Joy of Man's Desiring'. The whole effect is quite enjoyable but far from gripping.

'Home Truth', a despairing piece about marital breakdown sung to a deeply ironic 6/8 tempo, a rhythm more often associated with lively dances, displays little of the verbal gymnastics of many other songs – cartwheeling puns and trampolining paradoxes hardly appear. Because of this the song seems more heartfelt than the others, (though it is wrong to assume that complexity necessarily means insincerity, and even more misguided to assume that simplicity equals sincerity equals good). In fact 'Home Truth' is mediocre as *Goodbye Cruel World*'s songs go. The lyrics strain after effect but stumble. They're concerned, as the title suggests, with truth and lies, and the anguish and disorientation that arises from the blurring of the boundary between them. The narrator is so confused that he begins to lose the sense of his own identity. All in all it's a bleak, depressed and depressing song.

'Room With No Number' is one of the album's more interesting songs, evoking what ought to be typical Costelloland, a cheap hotel, but which is in fact found in surprisingly few songs – 'Motel Matches' and 'Man Out Of Time' are the only two that come immediately to mind. The 'plot' of the song is impossible to exactly pin down, but this is presumably intentional because the main theme is that of guilty suppression and confusion. The first verse describes a pair of lovers who to begin with seem to be happy and untroubled. Costello's lovers are rarely allowed such tranquillity, though, and we soon learn that they are 'hiding something' that 'no one must know', and indeed the listener is included in this injuction, for what they can't reveal is only the first of several mysteries. Love has created a 'terrible nightmare' for them, why and how we aren't told. In the last verse a girl arrives at the hotel who is apparently looking for the lovers, though we can only guess at her relationship with them.

The ambiguities of the song extend to its grammatical structure. The verses are clearly in the third person, concerning 'he', 'she' and 'they', but the chorus introduces 'you'. As often before this can be taken in two ways: either the lovers (or indeed someone else) are suddenly being addressed in the second person, or what appears to be the second person is really a colloquial version of the impersonal first person pronoun 'one'. There is no way of telling which is the 'correct' interpretation; if the latter is preferred then the narrator is not outside the events of the song, but involved in them, perhaps by being a guest at the hotel. Further complications arise in the middle where 'I' appears and where we learn that 'he was me'. This again is ambiguous, but what it seems to suggest is that the song's male lover is actually the narrator, who longs for a return to a simpler, better past. Thus a typically Costellian concern with time is mingled with an almost schizophrenic confusion of identity, and the mounting panic caused by this feeling of helpless depersonalisation is effectively echoed by the long instrumental section which ends the song, spinning around faster and faster like a crazy fairground ride heading for impending disaster.

The song relies quite heavily for its effect on the idea of a 'room without a number' probably inspired by numerous horror stories and films involving a concealed or locked room containing some nameless evil. In turn these stories owe something to the story of Bluebeard, who murdered his wives and kept their bodies in a locked room. It's not difficult to see that such stories are about the suppression of something that's feared but that's bound to have an evil effect however carefully it's hidden. In 'Room With No Number' we never discover the lovers' guilty secret. Have they broken the law? Are they eloping? Or is their shame related to sex? There's no way of telling, and consequently the song can be seen as concerning the guilty secrets and semiconscious anxieties everyone keeps in their cupboards and woodsheds.

'Inch by Inch', an ambiguous love song, contains one of Costello's occasional musical borrowings: the verses are founded on a near-replica of the bass riff from the Beatles' 'I'm Only Sleeping'. According to how charitable you're feeling this can be described as either a quotation or a shameless rip off. As I'm feeling in a moderately good mood at the moment I'll say that Costello quotes because the Beatles' song is about waking and dreaming, and there's a line in 'Inch by Inch', 'I just woke up from dreaming, I think', which throws a surreal veil over the song: is he awake or just dreaming he's awake?

The verses consist of lists of things, some of them quite unpleasant, that the narrator would allow his lover to do to him. It's implied that he will continue to love her despite them, but it's also suggested that she *does* in fact do some of these things. Hence the ambiguity of the love: it seems that she is yet another incarnation of the woman first encountered in 'Miracle Man' and, as we learn at the end of the last verse, she is trying to ditch him.

The first four songs offer personal reasons for saying goodbye to a cruel world, but the fifth, 'Worthless Thing', is a welcome return to public issues. It's an enjoyably vitriolic attack on the media, and in particular television and its incestuous relationship with the pop music industry. Costello savages those appalling game shows in which people are made to crawl before conveyor-belt idols in return for 'a split second of fame', and, in the chorus, attacks the media moguls for their arrogant disdain of everyone who doesn't match their conception of stardom.

Unscrupulous profiteers, whose 'eyes glint' with greed, who leech onto the lives and work of musicians (in particular Elvis Presley) also come under attack. They relentlessly trivialise their human subjects in order to turn them into marketable product, and Costello issues a blunt warning to anyone considering doing the same to him: 'Keep your bloody hands off my life'. Considering some of the sensational, spurious scandal that gets written about rock stars and other public figures I can appreciate his concern. I hope this present book can't be considered a similar exercise in cynical exploitation.

'Worthless Thing' is in some ways similar to 'Radio Radio', but lacks the earlier song's sheer venom. Still, it ranks as one of *Goodbye Cruel World*'s better songs. I'd like to be able to say the same of 'Love Field', (one of the album's four songs in 6/8 time, an unprecedentedy high number), but I think it ranks as an interesting oddity rather than a successful song. It's primarily a description of making love out of doors at night, and contains some awkward 'poetic' lines, which sound more like Cartland than Costello. Elsewhere it's more characteristically Costellian; despite the fact that it's fundamentally a love song there are several disturbing little details which seem to hint that the lovers' relationship is not a fully open and reciprocated one: she is 'sealed' and he is a 'functional stranger'. At the beginning of the song the woman is intimately addressed in the second person, but by the end she is simply referred to in the third: what starts as a song of pleasure in praise of honesty becomes a much more complex examination of anxiety and the extreme difficulty of reaching genuine intimacy.

'I Wanna Be Loved', an old soul song, is like a subtext to all Costello's personal songs. It's almost as if this is what he's been longing to say, but hasn't been able to bring himself to say it so straightforwardly, and needs the smoke screen of a cover version. It's by no means unpleasant to listen to, but it's not really what we expect from the author of, say, 'Man Out Of Time', which has a similar message. 'I Wanna Be Loved' is about as middle-of-the-yuppie-road as Costello has yet strayed: if 'Man Out Of Time' gets some of its effect from its seedy atmosphere, 'I Wanna Be Loved' exploits not the seedy but the CD.

'The Comedians' is a minor song about the emptiness of modern society. It's set in the 'motor car kingdom' (which perhaps makes it a Morris Minor song), where people succumb to the 'gentle persuasion' of consumerism. However, they discover that materialism is deluding and unfulfilling, by no means the first time we've heard of this idea.

If the lyrics seem like a halfhearted recycling of ideas that have been used to much better effect several times previously, the same can't be said of the music. This is so unusual that it comes as quite a shock to realise that the verses' time signature is 5/4

127

(moving seamlessly to 6/8 for the chorus). Five beats to the bar is a rare enough rhythm in any form of music, and is almost unknown in rock. There must be a few other examples, but Jethro Tull's 'Living in the Past' and the verses of the Beatles' 'Good Morning, Good Morning' are the only ones I can think of. This rhythm certainly adds variety to the album, and its awkward shambling gait successfully suggests the lack of inner tranquillity of the children of the motor age.

The 'plot' of 'Joe Porterhouse', like that of 'Room With No Number', is unclear, but involves a man having to leave his wife and children, possibly to go and serve in the forces. The precise reasons for their having to part remain very vague, however, and the song focuses upon the human drama of the situation: the children listening to their parents crying, the wife watching her husband sleeping peacefully before he leaves her, his distance from his family in a hot foreign country. Throughout the song runs an injunction to not 'let them see you crying that way'. This implies perhaps that a few decorous tears are acceptable, but that whole-hearted grief is tantamount to suggesting that the authorities are wrong to send Joe wherever they choose to send him. Emotions are always awkward for bureaucracies because they interfere with the smooth running of plans.

An earlier version of 'Joe Porterhouse', 'I Love You When You Sleep', recorded by Tracie, has the same chorus tune (and some of the same words) but completely different verses. It's a rather touching almost-love song, observing unoriginally but truthfully that even unpleasant people look vulnerable and innocent when asleep. It's surprising, though, that Costello chose to reuse the chorus, (which seems to me musically weaker than either version of the verse), especially the last two lines, the simple rise and fall of which sounds to me not very inspired.

'Sour Milk-Cow Blues' is another song in which the narrator laments his abandonment by his lover. The opening lines tell us that she likes coffee and tea more than she likes him. (With imagery like this, can the Nobel prize be far away?) It is an extremely ordinary song, surely one of Costello's weakest; only the vigour of the Attractions and the inventive production render it listenable. Its main interest is that it continues to play with the album's theme of disjointed identity: the narrator notes that his lover is 'different' and fancifully supposes that she has been replaced by a 'living double'. But to imply, however whimsically, that the reason she's losing interest in him is because 'somebody's putting ideas in [her] head', thus suggesting that she is incapable of thinking for herself, reveals an attitude to women that makes it hardly surprising that she'd rather have a nice cup of Nescafe than his patronising manner.

A handful of earlier songs, for example 'Big Tears' have dwelt on death – and 'The Great Unknown' is a further *memento mori*. Its construction is unusual but quite effective: the three verses are unrelated except that they are all concerned with various forms of death. The first is set in the criminal underworld, where some gangsters in traditional fashion set their victim's feet in concrete and drown him. The song effectively conjures up the semi-derelict industrial area and its oily river. The words 'lest we forget' (actually a quotation from Kipling's poem 'Recessional', but rooted in Biblical language) produce an appropriately elegaic atmosphere. The second verse also draws on the Bible, in the shape of the Samson and Delilah story (though taking an ironic look at Tom Jones' 'Delilah' in passing). It points out that even the rich and strong die, and tries to mingle the comic with the grisly physical details of death, described with macabre relish. Finally we are reminded of the multitudinous murders of the two World Wars. A bit of social criticism slips in as the 'VIPs [sing] "Wooden Heart" ', suggesting their jingoistic lack of compassion for the men they condemn to die, while 'The band [play] "Hearts of Oak" ', suggesting the ordinary soldiers' loyalty and humanity.

The verses just about succeed in unsentimentally but movingly approaching the engima of death. Given a clinching chorus, like that of many earlier songs, this would be one of the album's best songs. Unfortunately the chorus is anticlimactic, neither the tune nor the words measuring up to the admittedly difficult task. This is a pity: there are thousands of good rock songs about love, though not everyone falls in love, and hardly any about death, the only event we can all be sure of experiencing.

'The Deportees Club' is set in a nightclub, which could be in Rome, or in any other European or American city. Costello's point is the transnational characterlessness of such places: from Manhattan to Manchester, from Nice to Neasden, the tacky 'fibreglass ruins' theme decor is the same. The denizens of such places are lacking individuality, morality and any sense of purpose or direction. The chorus lists seven drinks from as many countries, suggesting a bewildering rootlessness. But to call the club patrons 'deportees' is of course deeply ironic: they are exiles not in the sense that they are political or war refugees, but because their jet-setting lifestyle denies them a genuine cultural identity. Their hedonism is an empty passing of time: on one hand 'time stand[s] still' for them because their lives are unchanging, but on the other time is simply meaningless, they have no sense of their place in history. So two of Costello's favourite themes, time and the vacuity of pleasure-seeking, are linked, and there's a further twist at the end where the narrator says 'I'm a deportee', implying either that he is just as guilty as everyone else, or that he has been so comprehensively fleeced that he is literally being deported. The innocent abroad comes a cropper once again.

Although this description of the song makes it sound quite powerful, in fact I can't help comparing it with 'Pump It Up', which is in many ways similar and far superior. The earlier song is exhilarating, while 'The Deportees Club' manages only a some-what synthetic excitement. Again Costello is repeating himself, a charge that can't be levelled at the final song, 'Peace In Our Time', which deals with an almost completely new theme (new to Costello, that is); nuclear war. This should be a subject right up his street. It hurts to say it, but the song doesn't work.

The opening verse invokes Neville Chamberlain after the signing of the Munich peace treaty of September 1938. But to equate these circumstances with the outbreak of a hypothetical Third World War is quite inappropriate. Chamberlain was trying to appease when clearly a moral (and consequently a military) stand was necessary; if a nuclear war does break out it will probably be because both sides are too aggressive and unwilling to compromise. Furthermore, Chamberlain, as far as I know, genuinely thought that he was making the best possible move, so to describe him as having 'a condemned man's stare' is to falsify history in a way already attacked in 'The Invisible Man'. Supporters of the song would say that the important parallel is that Chamberlain's belief that he had won 'peace in our time' was mistaken, and that the peace of today is equally illusory. That's true enough, but if you're going to use history to support your arguments you should make sure the comparison stands up to scrutiny and is not simply superficial.

The chorus is equally flawed. In order for a pun to work it must make sense on both (or all) levels. 'The bells take their toll' does not. Bells toll, yes, especially for a death, and the toll being taken suggests nuclear genocide, but to say 'the bells take their toll' is simply nonsense. Such a solecism in a crucial place in the song is a serious blemish.

I should have expected a song by Costello on this theme to focus on the effect of war on ordinary individuals (as 'Shipbuilding' does so successfully), but 'Peace In Our Time' makes almost no attempt to do this. Instead the last verse is devoted mostly to attacking President Reagan's messianic delusions, and even then the lines seem more like a routine denunciation, not something fired with real passion. All in all I find 'Peace In Our Time' deeply disappointing. The only touch of near genius is the trombone, the falling phrases of which are lugubriously beautiful; by a pleasing coincidence the trombone is sometimes used in classical music to symbolise the Last Trump, for example Mozart's *Requiem*.

By 1984 Costello had released an album of original material annually for eight years, and written well over a hundred songs, so with hindsight it was inevitable that sooner or later a marked decline was going to set in. No one could keep up such a level of fecundity while maintaining the highest standards for long. *Goodbye Cruel World* is one of Costello's weakest albums, possibly even his weakest. It contains no songs that I'd feel happy about including in a list of his best, and several quite bad ones. Still, for all that it's a recognisably quirky album, exhibiting many of Costello's recurrent themes, and as such is by no means without interest.

Predictably, there are no happy love songs. Some of them appear at first hearing to belong to this category, but as I've tried to show, this is illusory. In general the failure of relationships is still blamed on the fickleness of women (and in 'The Great Unknown' death is personified as female), though this isn't stressed as much as on some previous albums. Indeed, in 'Home Truth' Costello accepts that he is at least as much to blame as her. 'Worthless Thing' is a familiar attack on the media and modern commercial society in general, which is roughly the subject matter of 'The Comedians' and 'The Deportees Club'. The world's cruelty is exhibited in well-rehearsed forms.

This is probably the album's chief defect: too many of the songs are rehashes of earlier themes. While it's true that in one sense most of Costello's songs are rehashes because his subject matter is quite limited for such a prolific composer, this is usually not a problem because he so skilfully rings the changes and presents

131

new aspects of old themes. 'Shot With His Own Gun' and 'The Long Honeymoon', for example, are very similar in subject matter, but they're both very good songs nevertheless: the treatment of the subject matter is sufficiently varied for both to have independent lives of their own. But listening to, say, 'Home Truth', it's hard not to unfavourably compare it with 'Kid About It' and other much superior songs about disintegrating relationships.

Several songs, however, deal with new or nearly new subjects, in particular 'Room With No Number', 'Joe Porterhouse', 'The Great Unknown' and 'Peace In Our Time'. From the preceding paragraph the reader might assume that in my opinion the existence of these songs redeems the album. This is partially true, but I'd be a lot happier if these four songs did what they set out to do more effectively. 'Room With No Number' is cleverly constructed, though the tune is fairly rudimentary, but the other three, as I've already tried to demonstrate, give the impression of being unfinished and not properly thought out. Most of the *Goodbye Cruel World* songs were apparently written almost to order in a period of a couple of months or less. Most of Costello's songs give the illusion of being written quickly (because of their spur-of-the-moment white-heat intensity, and also because of the simple fact that there are so many of them), but there's a difference between writing songs quickly because important things need to be said *now*, and writing them quickly because there's an album to fill. I'm in danger of sounding snootily censorious here: Costello's most trivial throwaways are more substantial than most pop pap, but in order for my praise to be meaningful I've got to also criticise when I think it necessary. Although none of the *Goodbye Cruel World* songs is completely worthless, some of them seem to me to be written to formulae rather than urgently dictated by Erato and Euterpe, the muses of lyrics and music. They're a kind of instant song: take a freeze-dried theme, just add powdered imagery, mix with watery music, bake in the studio oven ('here's one I prepared earlier') and hey presto! Wholesome fare for all the family. The lyrics too often attempt dazzling feats of word-play that end up being slightly fumbled or that even miss the mark altogether, and there are no tunes that I find really memorable.

Despite these deficiencies the album has a classy, if in places glossy, sound which makes it quite entertaining listening. Credit for this must go partly to the producers, Clive Langer and Alan Winstanley, who keep Nieve's keyboards well to the fore after the relatively backseat role they'd given him on *Punch The Clock*. Their resourcefulness comes in particularly handy in 'Sour Milk-Cow Blues' and 'The Deportees Club', two musically uneventful songs that greatly profit from the bit of knob twiddling and tape effects, yet most of the songs are allowed to speak for themselves with only the minimum of interference.

After *Goodbye Cruel World* Costello did not release any more albums (except the *Best of* compilation) for over a year and a half – easily his longest absence from recording since the appearance of *My Aim Is True*, (though he did have a half-share in one pseudonymous single, 'The People's Limousine'). By the time of *King Of America* he had more or less dropped the name 'Elvis Costello' and reverted to his real name, Declan MacManus, but he continued to use a variety of other *noms de guerre* also. With the benefit of hindsight it's tempting to see hints of this radical rethink in *Goodbye Cruel World*'s theme of the disjointing of personality. Although it's true that right from the start of his career Costello experimented with names – 'Elvis Costello' is after all a pseudonym, and 'Stamping Ground', the B-side of 'You Little Fool', is eccentrically credited to 'The Emotional Toothpaste' – after this album this chameleon-like assumption of different names really took off. It's almost as if 'Home Truth', 'Room With No Number', 'Sour Milk-Cow Blues' and 'The Deportees Club' (and perhaps the occasional lines in other songs too) are dramatising his dissatisfaction with his 'Elvis Costello' persona. This blurring and fracturing of identity is also (perhaps coincidentally) displayed in the sleeve photos, which present enigmatic pictures of the musicians, not straightforward portraits. (The inner sleeve features a painting and a fragmented jigsaw of the same picture, which seems to make the same point.) We can guess that Costello (as I shall continue to refer to him, for the sake of convenience) was finding the strain of producing records, touring and leading a family life too great, it was tearing him up and tearing him down, and he needed a rest and a change. In order to make a new start you've first got to end, hence the farewell of the album's title. (Of course I don't mean to imply that the full implications of the title were intended at the time, after all he continued touring for months after the album's release, but in retrospect the title's appropriateness is just too neat to ignore.) 'I Hope You're Happy

Now' was announced as a forthcoming single, but symptomatically didn't appear. (It turned up eventually on *Blood And Chocolate*.) It was goodbye from Elvis Costello, but thankfully not goodbye from Declan MacManus.

Two other original songs appeared in 1984, one the B-side of 'I Wanna Be Loved', 'Turning the Town Red'. This highlights Costello's rather perverse tendency to release some of his best material in relatively obscure places: anyone else would have made such a strong song into a single, especially when it was the theme music of a TV series (Alan Bleasdale's *Scully*). The strong tune and attractive harmonies support a lyric which teeters between celebration and threat. To paint the town red means of course to go on a boisterous spree, but *turning* the town red, when seen in the light of some of the other quite sinister lines, evokes bloodshed. Consequently you're never quite sure how to take the song, and from this ambiguity it gets its vitality.

The other offcut from the workman's bench, 'Shatterproof', appeared on Billy Bremner's *Bash* album. This very Squeeze-like song, with its sorry tale of a young couple moving into a rented flat with high hopes, only to find them shattered, sounds as if it could well have been written several years earlier, possibly during the *Trust* period.

For the sake of completeness I'll mention the greatest hits compilation, *The Best of Elvis Costello – The Man*. Despite the rather absurd subtitle and cover art, this is a useful and not unbalanced collection. Most albums up to *Goodbye Cruel World* are fairly represented, though *Get Happy!!*'s best tracks are not included, and *Imperial Bedroom* is seriously undervalued. Still, with eighteen songs it's a good buy. It was released partly to fill Costello's otherwise uncomfortable recording silence, and was the last release to use unconditionally the name 'Elvis Costello'. (*Blood And Chocolate* is credited to 'Elvis Costello and the Attractions', but Costello himself is listed by his real name and another pseudonym.) So ends one phase of his career. The king is dead. Long live the king!

10

'King Of America'

The once prolific Costello, with about 130 original songs to his credit, released precisely one half of a new song in 1985. This was 'The People's Limousine', a vigorous burst of acoustic rocka-billy, co-written with T-Bone Burnett (who also appeared with Costello at his solo concerts in the same year). The single was credited to The Coward Brothers, Costello assuming for the occasion the jokey pseudonym Howard Coward. He also appeared as a guest vocalist on some other artists' albums, continued his production work and performed one song (the Beatles' 'All You Need Is Love') at the Live Aid concert. But despite this activity his admirers were used to hearing a lot more from him, and in particular were used to hearing new songs. This unprecedented silence brought the rumours crawling out of the dung-heap, for example that he was a drunken wreck who could no longer put two lines together, let alone write a decent song. I can remember, during this period, going into a record shop every now and again and looking through the Cs in the single-racks, hoping to find the latest release. Month succeeded month, but nothing appeared. What *was* the man playing at?

Consternation was increased when at last in early 1986 some-thing of interest to me finally appeared among the Claptons and the Commodores. This was 'Don't Let Me Be Misunderstood', which was a cover version of an old Animals' song. Despite the presence of an original (but lightweight) song on the B-side, this seemed to be a virtual confirmation of the rumours. If after more than a year and a half this was the best he could come up with something was definitely wrong. It wasn't that the single was especially bad – or bad at all – but to break such a protracted silence with a non-original was like a confession of creative sterility. A lot of people, including me, glumly assumed that this was the end of the road. After all, I reflected, rock music is a very limited art form – half a decade or so seems to be about the maximum span permitted to rock musicians in which they are really good, then they start parodying themselves, and Costello had arrived at that point.

Which just shows how wrong you can be. Soon after the single *King Of America* appeared, and immediately blew away the doubts. Here was the fruit of that lost year and a half, a collection of songs superior to the previous two albums. A few changes had taken place too. Most significantly, the words 'Elvis Costello' nowhere appear on the album (except on a removable sticker on the front of the sleeve, perhaps included at the insistence of the marketing men). It is credited to something called 'The Costello Show' (the inner sleeve adding 'featuring the Attractions and the Confederates'), and produced by T-Bone Burnett and a strange character called Declan Patrick Aloysius MacManus. Furthermore, a glance at the label on the record reveals that none of the songs are written by Costello, but that this MacManus chap turns out to be some kind of composer too. (And on the inner sleeve one of the guitarists is called 'The Little Hands of Concrete'.)

Something quite remarkable has happened. Previously quite defensive, even secretive, about his real name (though I've never been quite sure why a name one's given at birth is more 'real' than any other), Costello has more or less shed his meticulously contrived 'Elvis Costello' persona and been reborn as Declan Patrick Aloysius MacManus. (This adds 'Aloysius' to the name his parents gave him, so even now there's a little bit of showmanship involved. I wonder if this addition is a kind of indirect homage to the comedian Tony Hancock, who used it as part of his stage name, or a tongue in cheek attempt to make himself sound more cuddly by alluding to Sebastian Flyte's teddy bear in Evelyn Waugh's *Brideshead Revisited*.) This reversion to his real name signalled a dissatisfaction with the mask that he had worn for the previous eight or nine years, and a desire to face the world without a distorting intermediary.

He spoke about this in an interview in the *New Musical Express* soon after *King Of America*'s release: 'The losing of my name is just a little device to remind people that there was always a human being behind the funny glasses. For the first few records it was such an effective guise, a smokescreen for insecurities and a cover for the public learning process that was forced on me. But then I found that people couldn't rid themselves of their preconceptions and kept looking for things on the later records that just weren't there. Elvis Costello became more and more a character I *played* because people wouldn't let him grow up.'

It's obviously true that the angry young man persona of *My Aim Is True* was quickly outgrown, though the later Costello certainly inherited some of his characteristics. 'Elvis Costello' has not been static, but has evolved and matured, as people do, leaving behind many traits in the process. Now the point has been reached where the label 'Elvis Costello' is no longer an accurate description of the merchandise. As he remarked in a *Melody Maker* interview at about the same time, 'Elvis Costello's a brand name. Like Durex.' Had *King Of America* been sold as an Elvis Costello album, if anyone bought it expecting to find the old mixture of rage, cruelty, denunciations and despair then they might have felt inclined to prosecute under the Trades Descriptions Act.

This explains the death, or at least disappearance, of Elvis Costello, but the resurrection of Declan MacManus also calls for some comment. After all, it wouldn't have been impossible to exchange one stage name for another, but the reversion to his real name seems to be an attempt to reveal the 'human being behind the funny glasses'. Some of the earlier albums, especially *Get Happy!!* and *Imperial Bedroom*, have the appearance of being confessional, and *King Of America* takes this one stage further. This is not to say that the songs are directly autobiographical. Costello has always jealously guarded his personal life, and why shouldn't he. But although the album contains only a very few specifically autobiographical details, you can't help but notice that a new feeling of love and happiness shines out of several songs. This is especially apparent when compared with the weary jaundice of the previous album.

This sea-change in his outlook on life was partly the result of his newly formed relationship with Cait O'Riordan (who used to be the Pogues' bass-player) following his separation from his wife. The disappearance of Elvis Costello was like a burial of the traumas that had gone before, and the revival of his real name a token of sincerity and faith in the future. This revival implied that he was almost literally a new man, or to be more precise a young man again, since Declan MacManus was his name before the age of twenty-two, when the sordid world of rock music began to corrupt him. We can if we like see in his reversion to his real name another manifestation of his concern with time and nostalgia, as expressed in songs such as 'New Amsterdam' and 'Black And White World'. The resurrection of Declan MacManus is perhaps also an attempt to resurrect the (real or imagined) innocent happiness associated with the name. This might be trying to read too much into it, but what is undeniable is that the change of name signals the appearance of a more open, relaxed and cheerful Costello. (As I've already remarked, for simplicity's sake I'll continue to call him this.)

So much for the background – what of the album itself? The first impression given by the sleeve is that Costello, far from having returned to his humble roots, has let fame literally go to his head. He sports a large and vulgarly lavish crown, and the effect is absurd. Of course, it is intended to be absurd – a playful acknowledgement of the album's title and also of a line in 'I'll Wear It Proudly' in which he says that he'll gladly be crowned as the 'King of Fools'. Most of the previous sleeves have used a great deal of ingenuity in creating Elvis Costello's image, but now that image is mercilessly destroyed. You just can't take it seriously any longer having laughed at him in this ludicrous fancy-dress. This careless rejection of one of his main selling-points, that had taken years to lovingly create and nurture, was a brave move. When rock stars 'change their image', it usually means that they have a new hair-cut in a vague attempt to convince everyone that they've got something new to offer, but Costello's change is much more far-reaching. It's a tribute to his powers as an artist that his art survives it.

An even more fundamental change is that the Attractions, previously virtually inseparable from Costello's records, appear on only one of the fifteen tracks. You can dismiss all the other changes as mere window-dressing if you wish, but not this one. Although his songs are strong enough to stand up to almost any treatment, the Attractions have undeniably contributed vastly to their success. This change radically affects the sound of the record, and if proof were needed that Costello is sincere in his reorientation then this is it, for abandoning the sound that the record-buying public had come to associate with his name was a big commercial risk.

Replacing the Attractions is a selection of mostly veteran American musicians, including some who were members of the original

Elvis's band. Best known (to me) among them are James Burton, one of the great guitarists, who made his first record when Costello was only three, and the even greater Ray Brown, jazz bassist, who has played with such giants as Dizzy Gillespie and Duke Ellington. (Unfortunately, Brown appears on only two tracks.)

The album is very largely acoustic, quite unlike the aggressive electric style of the previous albums. Over two thirds of the songs include a double bass instead of a bass guitar, the rhythm guitar is almost exclusively acoustic rather than electric, and the studio technology of the three previous albums has just about gone – there's very little that couldn't have been performed live. Consequently it sounds fresh and spontaneous, even slightly rough at times, though never amateurish. This extends to the songs themselves, including the lyrics. Over the previous couple of albums his tortured clever-clever word-play had become in danger of disappearing up its own backside, becoming more and more contorted in its efforts to twist itself into staggering shapes. For *King Of America* Costello made a conscious decision to untangle himself. In the *Melody Maker* interview he said: 'It became clear to me that I had to write very, very simple songs. I started taking out all the musical kinks ... I was aware in retrospect that I hadn't been weighing the words properly, I hadn't been making them clear enough ... And suddenly in some way, I don't know why, it just seemed a lot easier for me to say something straight out.' Even though it's an exaggeration to call some of the songs 'very, very simple', it's true that on the whole they're more straightforward than very many earlier ones. For this reason some of them don't call for as much comment as those on previous albums, but this is no reflection on their quality.

The opening song, 'Brilliant Mistake', is virtually the album's title track. It concerns America, and it is by no means the first time that Costello has broached this subject. References to the USA are moderately frequent in his work, and have revealed a very ambivalent attitude to the country (see my discussion of the 'Dallas Version' of 'Less Than Zero', for example). 'Brilliant Mistake' pursues this theme; in the *NME* interview Costello explained that, 'No place on earth has ever been based on such high principles, principles that have either been betrayed or used to beat people around the head with.' The song explores the paradox of the contrast between the grand and honourable aspirations of the American Dream and the reality.

An even more recurrent theme of Costello's songs is that of illusion and deception, and this plays a big part in 'Brilliant Mistake'. America is presented as a country of 'broken dreams', where everything is artificial and brashly ostentatious. The woman in the second verse, for example, is implicitly criticised for her apparent boastfulness about her affairs, shocking to reticent English sensibilities. (Incidentally, in the same interview Costello castigated the English for seeing the Americans as rich and stupid stereotypes, a tendency this verse does nothing to dispel.) America is 'brilliant' because there's so much potential, but a 'mistake' because it's gone so horribly wrong.

The chorus is more personal. It returns to Costello's near-obsession with time, expressing a desire to be able to escape from the present back into the past. This applies both to America, because the early days of the nation were so superior to the Reagan era, and to Costello himself. I've already tried to show that his reversion to his real name is an escape to the safety of the past, and this theory seems to be confirmed here. At the end of the song the narrator/Costello/MacManus admits that he too is a 'brilliant mistake'; we have of course to live in the present, it's impossible to return to the past, so we are obliged to live with our failures and mistakes. As much as we'd like to we can't wipe the slate clean and start again, and the song's real strength is its unflinching recognition of this.

'Lovable' (co-written with Cait O'Riordan) is one of the album's uptempo numbers, and swings along infectiously. As its title suggests it's basically a love song, but by no means an entirely simple one. The *NME* interviewer dismissed it as 'self-explanatory', which underestimates its complexity. It doesn't just say 'I love you and you love me'. To begin with there's another woman and another man on the scene (as well as the narrator and his lover), suggesting rivalry. In addition, several of the narrator's compliments addressed to his lover are by no means straightforward. For example, the chorus remarks that news of her lovableness is circulating, a cynical reading of which would say that she has been spreading her favours around rather too liberally. The reference to 'bedlam' doesn't inspire confidence, and most disturbingly of all she is described as 'lifelike'. What on earth are we to make of this? This is to say the least an odd thing to say to

140

someone. Costello said that 'everything you *don't* understand is *exactly* what it appears to be'. In which case 'Lovable' is addressed to an inflatable rubber woman. Obviously it's not, but what this shows is that Costello can hardly help writing ambiguously even when he's trying to be simple. (I can't quite decide whether this is good, because it enriches his songs by mirroring ambiguous reality, or bad, because a good writer ought to be able to state things clearly and concisely when he wants to.) But leaving all speculation aside, 'Lovable' remains a goodish song about the complexity of love.

'Our Little Angel' is the latest in a long line of songs about siren-like women. The setting is a seedy emotionally sterile bar, the scene of many other songs. All this is almost tiresomely familiar to anyone who knows Costello's earlier work, but there is an enlivening twist. Instead of despising her and the lifestyle she leads, the narrator is quite protective towards her. While he's by no means unaware of her faults, he views her as a victim rather than a predator, and is therefore sympathetic. 'Our Little Angel' is far more human than, say, 'Stamping Ground', an otherwise very similar song.

'Don't Let Me Be Misunderstood' was first performed by Nina Simone, though the Animals' version is probably more familiar. It's not difficult to see why Costello chose to record it. Professions of sincerity have played a part in his work since the title of his first album, and the desire to communicate is clearly especially appropriate on an album where he's wearing his heart on his sleeve. It was a strange choice of single, though, and his melodramatically intense vocal delivery isn't entirely comfortable.

Goodbye Cruel World's 'Worthless Thing' is in part an attack on television game shows, and the terrific 'Glitter Gulch' renews the assault. It dissects with cruel accuracy the absurdity and loathsomeness of such programmes, with their 'personality' presenters whose sole claim to fame is that they are well known, and the ritual humiliation of the greed-possessed competitors. The male competitor is probably a light-hearted version of Costello's persona, for halfway through the song and show he rebels, preferring to keep his dignity by being an 'outlaw'; rather than submit to the bribery. His rebellion is witnessed live on television by the watching millions, and although it's not clear precisely what he does it's basically a comic version of the destruction of Sodom and Gomorrah. As these cities were destroyed in punishment for

141

their citizens' wickedness, the programme is disrupted to purge its corruption and decadence. So although superficially 'Glitter Gulch' is a humorous comment on one aspect of transatlantic culture, it becomes a symbolic assault on the whole of that culture.

On all his other albums unhappy songs greatly outnumber happy ones. On *King Of America* this is reversed, (though none of the songs are absolutely unambiguously happy). 'Indoor Fireworks' is easily the album's most depressed and depressing song, being a study of a disintegrating relationship. It uses thematic punning suggested by the title, the 'fireworks' being the couple's rows. Although their marriage is going up in smoke at least there's no hint of recrimination on either side, just regret. 'Indoor Fireworks', with its funereal music, is a hopelessly sad song and not one I'm very fond of.

So far the album, while new in manner and presentation, has dealt with fairly well-worn themes. 'Little Palaces', a documentary song about poor housing and its results, changes this. It's good to see Costello branching out, though I have to say that I have some reservations about the song. The 'little palaces' of the title are the high-rise blocks of flats erected with such high hopes but which have since proved to be so highly disastrous. They are the central image in a bitterly sardonic anatomy of Britain in the 1980s. They're described as 'the sedated homes of England', quite a good pun suggesting not only valium and glue-sniffing but also brainwashing by the media. Indeed, the second verse mentions a woman who's in tears over the antics of a soap opera but is oblivious to the plight of her own family. The sections of the song depicting a vandalised soulless wasteland are powerfully effective.

The sections I'm not so happy about are those dealing with child-battering. There's no reason why Costello shouldn't write a song on this subject, but in my opinion he's confused the issue by mixing it up with the problem of sub-standard housing. In the *NME* interview he opined that there can be no excuse for hitting children, an opinion with which it's easy to agree. But in this case why bring in this subject at all? The song doesn't seem to know where its sympathies lie – on one hand it blames the flats, but on the other won't accept this as an excuse. This confusion is, I think, a blemish. Neither do I like the way he sings 'knock' – he sounds as if he's striving for effect instead of letting the song speak for itself – and the inversion of the name 'Pope John' solely for the sake of the rhyme is not evidence of a lyricist on top form. Many intelligent critics regard 'Little Palaces' as one of the album's triumphs, but I find it a bit too earnest for my taste. Some much needed self-deprecating levity could have been injected by the simple expedient of raising the key a semitone so that the song would be set in A flat.

'I'll Wear It Proudly' is a love song, though like 'Lovable' not a straightforward one. It well conveys the narrator's passionate desire to be with his lover, and in the chorus his willingness to abase himself for her. He would even endure ridicule by proudly wearing the crown of the 'King of Fools', thus openly admitting his earlier stupidity in relationships. An odd feature of the chorus is that he says she's stood him on his head (a goodish way of expressing being made to see the world completely anew) and nailed his feet in position. As well as being a somewhat bizarre image this sounds as if he's identifying with St Peter, who was crucified upside-down. The possibilities this opens up, especially considering Costello's nominally Catholic upbringing, are just too awesome to contemplate.

Side two begins with a couple of songs on specifically American themes. The first of these, 'American Without Tears', is in danger of having an extremely unCostellian word applied to it; 'charming'. It's the story of a visit to America during which the narrator meets two GI brides who left England after the war and are now middle-aged. Although the song still gets in a few swipes at the US (describing it as a land of 'lies', for example) its main purpose is to celebrate the women's vitality. The story of their first meeting with the GIs is told with real affection, and the soldiers are no longer seen as stereotyped thugs (as on *Armed Forces*) but as ordinary likable human beings. The chorus plays on the semi-proverbial phrase 'French without tears', implying that by leaving England they have left behind all worries and sorrows, easily the most positive image of the US to be found anywhere in Costello's work. It's a delightfully warm song, the slightly awkward waltz tune capturing his good-natured, warm-hearted response to the women.

The final verse and chorus are more personal. The narrator is apparently trying to get away from his lover, but admits that she is his true love even though he can't express this in words. But like the women he has been revived by America and now he too can speak 'American without tears'. The new world has brought him new life, as a new love brings a sense of resurrection. The joy is obvious, but is beautifully undercut by the chorus's mention of the 'crying' associated with the past, giving the song just an edge of melancholy. This bitter-sweet flavour makes it perhaps the album's most moving song.

From a celebration (albeit not a blind one) of the American Dream, to a denunciation of the Nightmare. This is blues singer J B Lenoir's 'Eisenhower Blues', which looks at the America of the 1950s from the point of view of the underprivileged, and is not impressed with what it sees. The inclusion of this song balances 'American Without Tears' by implying that America hasn't changed much in some respects in the last thirty years. I'd like, though, to hear a song written by Costello on this theme.

'Poisoned Rose' might be perversely described as an unambiguously ambiguous love song, because the ambiguity of the love is clearly its subject. The title reflects this, a rose being of course a symbol of beauty and purity, but if it's 'poisoned' this suggests that its beauty is a trap set to lure the unwary. This is a fine image of the narrator's predicament – he can neither live with nor without his lover, the beauty drawing him irresistibly, the poison repelling him. In the end he carries on even though this means swallowing his pride and grasping the thorns, and the result is an exquisite song. It's the only one in which bass player Ray Brown really gets the opportunity to show what he can do, and Costello gives what is for my money his best vocal performance on the record.

The intense silence that follows 'Poisoned Rose' is broken by the album's lightest song, the appropriately titled and highly enjoyable 'The Big Light'. A rueful reflection on the hangovers and indiscretions that result from drinking too much, it hasn't got any big ambitions but does what it sets out to do perfectly. There's one cheeky in-joke embedded in the lyric. The narrator wakes after a Bacchanalian night and can't bring himself to look at the 'Haggard face' of the woman he's drunkenly slept with. The capital 'H' in the printed lyric confirms that this is a sly reference to Rider Haggard, author of *She*, the story of Ayesha, She Who Must Be Obeyed, the archetype of the domineering woman who has featured in not a few of Costello's songs. It's good to see that he is capable of joking about this aspect of his work. (There's a similar joke in 'American Without Tears' – as the women lure the men a siren sounds, alluding to the mythological sirens who lured men to destruction with their song.)

144

The album's final love song is 'Jack of All Parades', and seems to be unusually directly autobiographical, for it's about the surrender of fame for the sake of love. The chorus, for example, balances the 'thrill' of being in the public eye with 'the love of one true heart', and the latter wins hands down. Normally I'm impatient with songs about the (no doubt very real) problems of being a rock star, because they seem self-indulgent. The ordinary non-famous listener is excluded from the songs, which are really just an excuse for disguised boasting. But 'Jack of All Parades' is an exception because the narrator's willingness to sacrifice everything for love is so obviously sincere, and the fame really doesn't mean all that much to him. The crucial part of the song, the last verse, makes no attempt to dress up his declaration of love in fancy lyrics – its simplicity and sheer ordinariness is convincing and somehow very touching. The thought that he, the master of word-juggling, failed just like the rest of us to make a big success of his proposal is comforting. We feel better about ourselves, and about him.

'Suit of Lights' is in some ways a companion piece to 'Jack of All Parades', for it also ponders the pressures of fame. Of all the songs on the album it's the one most directly concerned with Costello's personal history, and ironically enough is the one on which his long-standing partners the Attractions play. It's a kind of parable about the death of Elvis Costello, and by implication the rebirth of Declan MacManus, though there's nothing in the song so specific as this. (In interviews he confirmed that this interpretation was the one he intended.) The 'he' of the story, the Costello-figure watched dispassionately by MacManus, leads a stale and weary life. His songs are simply a waste of breath, and thinking back to the previous album, *Goodbye Cruel World*, with its suitably moribund title, it's hard to disagree. Consequently he metaphorically dies on stage (by being booed off it, perhaps). But then he is 'pulled . . . out of the cold, cold ground' and dressed in a 'suit of lights' (a dazzlingly ostentatious stage costume covered with hundreds of light-reflecting buttons). This is obviously an image of resurrection, but I'm not sure if it is intended to apply to the enforced, mechanical churning out of an Elvis Costello record in 1984 just to keep the punters happy, or the revival of Declan MacManus and *King Of America*. If the latter is intended then it doesn't quite work, because MacManus, far from wearing gaudy and distracting fancy dress, is exposing himself more nakedly than ever before.

So far this is all very self-referential, and doesn't mean much to the average person who isn't terribly interested in the details of Costello's life. If you like, though, you can see 'Suit of Lights' as a symbolic version of the ups and downs that all our lives go through, and of the renewing power of love. Also embodied in it are several typical cynicisms about the nature of the world. For example, the beginning of the second verse attacks the reactionary opinions of some sections of the press, and the last verse contains a casual glimpse of a brutal tar and feathering. This suggests that, as in 'Man Out Of Time' and several other songs, the world is a dangerous and hostile place, and the only way of gaining strength in order to face it is to experience love's regeneration.

Costello explained the album's last song, 'Sleep of the Just', in the *Melody Maker* interview: 'It's about hypocrisy. It's just about a soldier whose sister is a porno model and he's standing there all proud and full of himself in his uniform and looking down on her, and all the time, it's her picture that's up on the barracks' wall. It's very simple.' Well, he might think it's simple, but I couldn't have deduced all this just from the song. Having read his footnote, however, it becomes clear enough, though there are still some obscure passages. Quite how the second verse, with its apparent reference to terrorism, fits in I don't know. But this is intended to be a song with a moral. Both brother and sister are ashamed of each other's profession, though neither of them is morally superior to the other. So I suppose that the conclusion that we're intended to draw is that we shouldn't judge and dismiss other people, because we've all got our faults. This is a suitably forgiving note for such a humane album to end on, supported by a gently cautionary tune. *King Of America* is Costello's least condemnatory record. He recognises his own failings and is penitent, and is consequently not nearly so quick to criticise as previously.

Having said this, and although it remains true that *King Of America* is in many ways a new departure for Costello, few if any of the lyrics come as a big surprise to anyone who has closely followed his work. People whose attitude to him fossilised at the time of *Armed Forces* seven years earlier are going to be taken aback, it's true, but otherwise everyone will recognise the gradual evolution of his songs. I've already summarised the development of his persona up to the time of *Imperial Bedroom* (see pages 107–8), so I'll continue the story from there. After the impasse of this album – yearning for love but seeing little chance of getting it – the next two albums chase their own tails rather than making any real progress. Consequently they're both rather a mishmash. The narrators don't seem to know what to try next, and so try a bit of everything in the vague hope of making something work. *Punch The Clock* veers wildly between praise of marriage ('The Greatest Thing') and vilification of families ('The World And His Wife') and between outrage ('Pills And Soap') and resignation ('Shipbuilding'). Women are both pleaded with ('Mouth Almighty') and brutally beaten ('TKO'). The narrators don't know which way to turn, and by the time of *Goodbye Cruel World* still haven't found a point of rest. They try to cope with their loneliness by shrugging it off ('The Only Flame in Town') but find it impossible to maintain this front for long ('I Wanna Be Loved'). The relative failure of both these albums derives from their lack of direction.

The breakthrough comes in *King Of America*. At last the love that's been longed for has been attained, and this gives the album a tremendous sense of purpose. It's not an idyllic love and it brings its own problems with it, but nevertheless it's real. A surprisingly small proportion of the tracks are actually love songs (four out of fifteen), but their influence is felt throughout. Most of the songs find things to celebrate rather than denigrate: only three are thoroughly negative ('Indoor Fireworks', 'Little Palaces' and 'Eisenhower Blues'). Even 'Glitter Gulch', which begins as a misanthropic blast, ends in triumph for humanity. (It's instructive to compare this with the surrender at the end of the similar 'Worthless Thing' from the previous album.) Although there are still a few tongue-lashings lurking in the album's darker corners, and the narrators are evidently not easy people to live with, they're a lot *nicer* than before. You wouldn't be apprehensive of introducing them to your mother. We've come a long way since the knock-kneed pigeon-toed scowling figure on the front of *My Aim Is True*. He would have sneered at her hairstyle, mocked her dress sense and then expected to be asked to stay for tea.

It's love that makes the difference to *King Of America*, but fortunately Costello doesn't forget public issues. Several songs, especially 'Brilliant Mistake', 'Glitter Gulch', 'Little Palaces' and 'Eisenhower Blues', show that he is not too busy staring in his lover's eyes to remember the world around him. Earlier public songs are largely occupied in identifying the sinister Mr Bigs who are behind the scenes and manipulating everyone else. Although there are still vestiges of this somewhat paranoid explanation of the world's inequalities and injustices, on the whole the conspiracy theory has been abandoned, and replaced by the rather more lenient cock-up theory. For example, 'Little Palaces' makes no attempt to claim that high-rise flats were built as a means of getting the working classes out of the way. They were built with good intentions, but have turned out horribly wrong. So Costello's new-found benevolence even extends almost as far as the men with the tickertape.

King Of America is undoubtedly a good album, especially when measured against its two disappointing predecessors. I don't think I'd quite allow it equal ranking with *Get Happy!!*, *Trust* and *Imperial Bedroom*, but it's not far behind. Costello has something new to say (along with plenty of familiar things) and finds a new way of saying them. Content and form are in harmony, and the result is an extremely satisfying record.

This chapter has to end anticlimactically with two very ordinary songs, both reverting to the theme of the coquette but with little of the sympathy or insight of 'Our Little Angel'. 'Baby's Got a Brand New Hairdo' (great title), the B-side of 'Don't Let Me Be Misunderstood', is performed with the Attractions. It's taken at a hectic pace and wouldn't sound out of place on side two of *This Year's Model*. 'Shoes Without Heels' was not released until 1987 on the twelve-inch version of 'Blue Chair', but was recorded during the *King Of America* sessions. Its lachrymose tale would have perfectly suited *Almost Blue*. If *King Of America* is intended to be a warts and all portrait of the 'human being behind the funny glasses' then I suppose these two songs count as warts.

11

'Blood And Chocolate'

One of Costello's great strengths has been that he rarely goes backwards. Both lyrically and musically nearly all his albums are different from their predecessors, and over the decade of his recording career he has experimented with a number of different styles. He doesn't complacently repeat successes, but tries to avoid becoming stale by pressing on into new territory. Nowhere is this more evident than on *King Of America*, which is a radical progression from his earlier work. You would expect, then, that his next album would take up from where *King Of America* left off and continue from there, developing the themes and styles so as to create a new amalgam. In particular you'd probably expect it to build on the newly won positive outlook on life. Strangely, this wasn't what happened.

Blood And Chocolate must have been recorded almost straight after the release of the previous album, because it appeared just a few months later. Maybe Costello didn't give himself enough time to think about it and prepare it, but for whatever reason it's disappointing. There are few signs of any progress, and if anything it's a retrogressive album. The joy of *King Of America* has evaporated and we're back with songs and sentiments that could have come from the first three albums.

Symptomatic of this retreat is the fact that the album is credited to 'Elvis Costello and the Attractions' (though only on the front of the sleeve and the label on the record). His hard-won new identity, with its associations of open-heartedness, has been partially surrendered. It's true that the name 'MacManus' survives as composer of all but one of the songs, but much more prominent is the silly pseudonym 'Napoleon Dynamite'. This is the name that appears under Costello's photograph on the back of the

149

sleeve, and in all the musicians' credits. Furthermore, the ugly (and rather phallic) painting on the front is entitled 'Napoleon Dynamite'. Costello's other two changes of name – from MacManus to Costello and back again – have had good reasons behind them, but this change strikes me as being simply an irritating gimmick. Having some of the record's credits printed in Esperanto also seems to be a random attempt to draw attention. The packaging of most of the other albums is well conceived and throws light on the contents, but in *Blood And Chocolate*'s case it's scraping the bottom of the barrel for ideas.

One aspect of the sleeve that is a true reflection of the record is Costello's photograph. This shows him mouth agape in a hammy angst-ridden scream. This wouldn't have been out of place on the deeply unhappy first four albums, and shows his persona reverting to a previous incarnation. As the title of one of his earlier songs has it, this is a case of 'Five Gears In Reverse'.

To some extent, however, we can welcome this regression. The Attractions return, and so does producer Nick Lowe, in charge of a Costello album for the first time since *Trust*. Consequently, although the substance is thin, at least there's a superficial vitality and energy. Organs and electric guitars are once again the dominant instruments, giving the album a sound reminiscent in places of *This Year's Model*.

The opening song, 'Uncomplicated', is an oddity. It's a kind of 'love' song, but I put 'love' in quotation marks because other contradictory emotions are present too. Disgust, revenge and sleazy passion are all mixed up together. The first line, which gives the album its title, suggests violence and sickly sweetness, opposed concepts to match the confused feelings of the narrator. The words 'blood and chocolate', taken with the rest of the song, bring to my mind a scene in which a woman clutches a box of Black Magic after having been hit by her vengeful lover. A sense of vicious threat hangs over the song, which is enhanced by the curious music. The first three beats of each bar are heavily accented, the fourth unaccented, creating a lumbering, brutal effect. What's more, the verses are sung entirely on one chord, giving a feeling of monotony and claustrophobia. All in all it's most unpleasant, especially as the narrator taunts his lover with the knowledge that worse is going to follow.

'I Hope You're Happy Now' (which dates from 1984) is musically and lyrically not unlike 'No Action'. Both are denunciations of the narrator's ex-lover and her new partner, and are fired by scorn and contempt. The difference is that the earlier song is only using these feelings to provide a smokescreen for the narrator's emotions – desire and regret – while in 'I Hope You're Happy Now' he is genuinely glad to be rid of her. This is one of the album's most enjoyable songs because of its liberating gleefulness, though it's a shame that the benevolence of *King Of America* should have degenerated into these snide jibes. The message of 'Sleep of the Just' has been all too quickly forgotten.

'Tokyo Storm Warning' is probably Costello's longest ever song (to be precise, it was co-written with Cait O'Riordan). It's a catalogue song, lacking narrative or any other form of unity except that all its imagery is devoted to detailing the less appealing aspects of the world in the 1980s. Not all of the images make sense on a literal level, but this adds to the nightmarish and hallucinatory quality. In fact the mood is best described as apocalyptic. The first verse mentions 'hell', and is signalled in the opening words, 'the sky fell' (reminding me a little of the first line of Dylan's 'It's All Right, Ma, I'm Only Bleeding': 'Darkness at the break of noon', a song with which 'Tokyo Storm Warning' has some similarities). The world is described as being in the grip of utter anarchy, with no sense of purpose or morality. So in the chorus everyone treats life as a 'joke', hedonism being the only response to its meaninglessness. People don't even consider the future consequences of their actions, living only for today, and so there's little chance of the world improving.

'Tokyo Storm Warning' (Tokyo perhaps because Costello regards Japan as an awful example of what can happen when capitalist consumerism is allowed to run riot) contains plenty of good lines, but the music is unable to sustain the listener's interest for the mammoth duration. It's very simple and not very original. The tune is a close relation of Chuck Berry's 'Memphis', the rhythm guitar chugs up and down through sixths and sevenths as in a thousand other rock songs, the riff from the Rolling Stones' 'Satisfaction' whinges away in the background (probably as an intentional allusion), and the guitar solo sounds like one of George Harrison's out-takes from *circa* 1966. After this hotch-potch the end of the world might come as a relief.

'Home Is Anywhere You Hang Your Head' has one of the album's better tunes, but like 'Uncomplicated' returns to the view of women propounded by the early albums. The song is a portrait

151

of a man who's been abandoned by his lover, and it's hinted that she hasn't just left him but heartlessly and ruthlessly rejected him. This inspires Costello to a cynicism about relationships ('He's contemplating murder again/He must be in love') that verges on self-parody. Again we wonder where *King Of America*'s faith in love has gone. I'm not suggesting, of course, that Costello shouldn't ever write a song about an unhappy affair again, but to see him returning to territory already more than adequately explored is frustrating.

The theme of being abandoned by a woman is pursued in 'I Want You'. Costello evidently thinks well of this song since it was released as a single, and I know several intelligent listeners who regard it as ranking with his best, but I find it almost imposs-ible to listen to. It begins quietly with just an acoustic guitar for accompaniment, as if it's going to be a sincere love song (which I suppose it is, though not in the way you normally expect a love song to be sincere). Already the intensity of the narrator's love is apparent, but exactly what form it takes is not revealed until the electric bulk of the song begins. It becomes a study in smouldering jealousy, resentment and possessiveness. It quotes the lyric and tune of the Beatles' 'I Want You (She's So Heavy)' from *Abbey Road*, another song about obsession bordering on madness, thus intensifying the listener's sense of the narrator's near-derange-ment. The title is repeated incessantly as the narrator masochist-ically imagines his ex-lover with her new partner, and this certainly is not intended to be easy listening. The green-eyed monster has got him by the throat and it's not a pretty sight or sound.

Side two's opener, one of the livelier songs, is also about jeal-ousy, but this time it's her turn to feel the pangs. The scenario of 'Honey, Are You Straight or Are You Blind?' seems to be this: the narrator's relationship is in trouble because his lover is jealous of a real or imagined liaison between him and another woman. He indignantly denies this, but still she wants to tear her supposed rival apart. However, the song can be read in another way too, though I'm not sure if this is intentional. 'Straight' can of course mean heterosexual, and if you follow this lead you'll find that the reason that the relationship is on the rocks could be that she is sexually attracted to the other woman. In which case the chorus asks her if she realises this, and this is a song on an unusual theme.

152

'Blue Chair' also has an implicit story behind it: two men (one of them the narrator) are together, perhaps in a pub. The narrator's lover has fallen for the second man, who has just broken this news to the narrator. The interesting thing about this song, apart from its enjoyable pop tune, is that the narrator, far from abusing and despising his rival as in all the other songs, expresses support for and solidarity with him. Having said this there's not much to add. 'Blue Chair' is a moderately touching song about facing up to sudden and unexpected loss with dignity, and a welcome corrective to 'Home Is Anywhere You Hang Your Head' and 'I Want You'.

So far all but one of the songs ('Tokyo Storm Warning') have been personal, but 'Battered Old Bird' helps to expand the album's horizons. This is a description of the inhabitants of a run-down boarding house; they're all wrecks and misfits in one way or another, and you can if you like see the song as a symbol of Britain, though there's nothing in the song to signal that this is Costello's intention. The 'battered old bird' (my dictionary defines 'old bird' as 'wary person') of the title is representative of the inhabitants. He's cut off from the world both by living on an upper floor and by living in a pill-induced limbo. Another lodger decapitates a child and then tries to commit suicide, another is a so-called dirty old man. Even allowing for the fact that some of this is presumably surrealistic they're a pretty unsavoury bunch. In a smaller way 'Battered Old Bird' is every bit as apocalyptic as 'Tokyo Storm Warning': if its characters are representative of humanity then there's little hope for the world. They are all products of post-war Britain, and the song shows how they've been shoved to the side of life, as in 'The Invisible Man'. It makes no attempt to sermonise, but the song implies that we should have grave doubts about a system that causes so much wastage of humanity. (Incidentally, is the second middle, about the 'Macintosh Man', an allusion to Ian McEwan's compulsively repellent story 'The Cupboard Man', from *First Love, Last Rites*?)

'Crimes of Paris' is easily the album's most cryptic song. To begin with, what *are* the 'crimes of Paris'? (This phrase also appears in 'Jack of All Parades'.) Paris is notorious for its eroticism, so they could be immoral deeds fuelled by lust. Or could Paris be the mythological Paris, whose elopement with Helen of Troy precipitated the Trojan War? As both these readings suggest, the song is basically another dissertation on the theme of troubled relationships, though enlivened by a pleasantly sing-along chorus.

Costello's pseudonym on *Blood And Chocolate* is Napoleon Dynamite. One of the associations of the name Napoleon is over-confidence and self-importance. Costello must know this, and I assume and hope he's adopted the name ironically. There's little sign of this in the next song, 'Poor Napoleon', though. Is this, as it appears to be, a plain cry of self-pity? If so, it's embarrassing. Even if there is some subtle irony the quality of the song is enough to make John Denver blush. It's the feeblest number on what is arguably Costello's weakest album. It sounds like Val Doonican after taking an overdose. It strives to be blistering but scarcely raises an itchy rash. The only point of interest is that even though Costello sings it the narrator could be female, the only one of his songs written in this manner. As in several of the previous songs on the album, sexual jealousy is a theme.

Another way in which *Blood And Chocolate* is a retrogression is that like the early albums it contrives to end with its weakest songs, rather than saving up the best ones for a big climax. 'Next Time Round' is better than 'Poor Napoleon', but it's not in the same league as 'Big Sister's Clothes' or 'Town Cryer'. It's the umpteenth song about a woman who has left the narrator. The beginning of the lyric is very similar to that of 'I'm Not Angry' from the first album, which is not so much regression as recidivism. The narrator is listening as she makes love with her new boyfriend, but he still wants her and, as in 'I Want You', neurotically pores over his memories. The chorus is also characteristic of Costello's writing as he reminds her that he's going to die, and it's with this unarguably correct but macabre thought that the album ends.

Blood And Chocolate is Costello's tenth album of original songs recorded as a unit, (in other words, *Ten Bloody Marys* and the *Best of* set, compilations of songs written at different times, and *Almost Blue*, which wasn't written by Costello, are excluded). For a decade, from *My Aim Is True* in 1977 to *Blood And Chocolate* in 1986, he released on average an album per year (plus plenty of other bits and pieces, some of high quality). Many of the hundred and fifty or so songs written during this time are unquestionably as near to the status of masterpieces as rock songs are ever likely to get. It's a shame that the main part of this book has to end so anticlimactically. *Blood And Chocolate* vies with

154

Goodbye Cruel World for the unenviable title of Costello's worst album (I'd say that *Goodbye Cruel World* is marginally the better of the two, since at least it has a fair amount of thematic variety.) Both suffer from being the product of an overworked and temporarily threadbare inspiration, though it remains a mystery why Costello felt it necessary to rush out *Blood And Chocolate* so hard on the heels of *King Of America*. Surely it would have been better to wait until his powers had recuperated after a rest.

As I've tried to show, what makes the album so disappointing is that not only is there little that's new on it, but also there's so much that's nearly ten years old. In particular the songs about relationships — which make up the bulk of the album — are distinctly stale and mouldy. Women are again seen as spiteful viragos. The words I used to describe the way they're presented on *My Aim Is True* — fickle, bitchy and domineering — have become relevant once more. About half the songs are about being abandoned by a woman, though the narrators now openly admit their sorrow, unlike before. Compare 'I Want You' with 'Alison', for example. Both songs imply more or less the same story, but in the 1977 version the narrator never specifically makes clear his desire, his sadness, his longing, his jealousy — it's all in the subtext, in the music, in the atmosphere, and the result is beautiful, a marvel of unvoiced implications. In 1986, however, he says it very clearly — and says it, and says it, and says it. All subtlety has gone.

Furthermore, the album contains only two public songs, fewer than on any other LP except *Imperial Bedroom*. Although these two are among the album's more interesting songs they're not strong enough, and there aren't enough of them, to compensate for the weakness of the personal songs. I'd hoped that having got his personal life apparently sorted out Costello would have turned his attentions more frequently to the wicked ways of the world, but I hoped in vain.

There are only eleven songs on *Blood And Chocolate*, and as we've become used to the riches of *Imperial Bedroom* and *King Of America* (fifteen songs each), not to mention *Get Happy!!* (twenty), we're being short-changed. And although the album contains one less song than *My Aim Is True*, it lasts about half as long again. Previously one of Costello's virtues as a songwriter has been his precision and conciseness — things are said neatly, the point is made, and the song ends. But now there's a verbosity, all the more hard to accept because apart from the occasional line here and there the lyrics fail to inspire.

In case this is too harsh a judgment on the album perhaps I should add that some of my friends who are too young to remember what I regard as the cream of Costello from the early eighties, and are only familiar with his later work, are still admirers. Maybe my discontent with the album comes from my unfair expectation that he can maintain these supreme standards even after the circumstances that conspired to produce them are long gone.

And that's the end of the main plot of our story so far. A sadly subdued conclusion after the highlights of many of the preceding episodes. As I write this in the summer of 1988 there's no sign of a continuation – Costello has not released an album of new songs since 1986, a silence of over two years, longer even than that separating *Goodbye Cruel World* and *King Of America*. However, although the main plot has reached a hiatus, the sub-plot continues. Now read on . . .

In 1987 'Blue Chair' was released as a single, in a different, more soulful version than that on the album. On the B-side was 'American Without Tears No. 2 (Twilight Version)', a radical reworking, with completely new lyrics, of the fine song from *King Of America*. Also dating from 1987 is 'Seven Day Weekend'. This is co-written and performed with veteran Jamaican musician Jimmy Cliff (composer of the classic 'Many Rivers To Cross'), and is Costello's third tilt at the problem of unemployment. Both these tracks appear on *Out Of Our Idiot*, a collection along the same lines as *Ten Bloody Marys*. The eccentric title, implying that Costello is wise enough to play the fool (and an 'idiot' is a Sufi sage, though this is probably a coincidence), embraces seventeen songs not otherwise available on an album. Although not as good as the previous compilation its quality is high. For some reason 'Party Party' and 'Big Sister' are not included, (several good cover versions are omitted, too, such as 'Night Time'), but nevertheless unless you've already got most of the songs on singles it's an essential addition to a Costello collection.

Costello's music has featured in several films, and one song, 'Big Nothing', is included on the soundtrack album of *Straight to Hell* under the name 'The MacManus Gang'. This movie, a spoof cowboy film, was possibly even more disastrous than the others. The critics gave this spaghetti western a right pasting.

Of rather more interest is the soundtrack of *The Courier*. The album has one side of songs by groups such as the Hothouse Flowers and Something Happens, while most of side two consists of instrumentals composed by Costello (although he's credited as Declan MacManus – if you weren't in on the backstage story you'd never know that Costello was involved). He's never written, or at least never recorded, any instrumentals before, so eight of them all at once is a surprising diversification. The tracks experiment with a number of different styles and moods. They range from the Philip Glassish serial music for string orchestra of 'Mad Dog', through the hip-hop inspired rhythms of 'Rat Poison', to the atmospheric solo piano (played by Steve Nieve) of 'Furinal Music'. To be honest they don't stand up to repeated hearings, though 'Last Boat Leaving' shows Costello hasn't lost the knack of occasionally writing a good tune. Of course they're intended to be heard in the context of the film, which I haven't seen, and as such they sound no better and no worse than ninety-five per cent of other film background music. Several of the tracks feature British jazz musicians (although they aren't given the opportunity to show their paces) such as Guy Barker, Phil Todd and Don Weller, probably best known for their association with the wonderful Stan Tracey.

Costello's most recent appearance of all on record is another collaboration, with Rubén Blades, the salsa singer. Blades' album *Nothing But the Truth* (which also contains contributions from Lou Reed and Sting) features two songs co-written by Blades and Costello. The first, 'The Miranda Syndrome', is, according to Blades' sleevenote, about 'how the world has been fooled by stereotypes and false promises'. Add to this the lyric's slighting references to America and the media, and you have a recipe for a typical Costello song. The second, which also, according to the sleevenote, was written almost entirely by Costello, is called 'Shamed Into Love'. This is very beautiful; it risks a slightly slushy cabaret manner but gets away with it. It's the song of a man who realises, almost to his surprise, that he loves his wife, and who gives praise that she has rescued him from a permanently twisted view of the world. It's easily his best song since *King Of America*, gives us some reason to have hopes for his artistic future, and allows me to end this chapter on a high point.

12

A Man Out Of Time

I began this book with the assertion that Costello is one of rock's finest songwriters, and I hope that I have gone some way towards justifying this claim. Although his commercial popularity has never regained the peak it reached in 1979, he retains a dedicated following. His peers, other rock musicians, widely regard his songs as paragons of their art. Every intelligent listener, even if they find his music not to their personal taste, has to concede his ability as a composer. His reputation rests not only on the quality of his best songs but on their quantity too. Many rock musicians produce one or two excellent albums, but most burn out their talent distressingly quickly. Only the greatest of them manage to overcome the genre's limitations and continue to produce records that aren't simply cheap parodies of their earlier work. Costello surely is one of these few.

He has released a round dozen albums of original songs, at least three of which are in my opinion among the most quintessential rock records ever made – *Get Happy!!*, *Trust* and *Imperial Bedroom*. Another two are just on the fringes of this status – *My Aim Is True* and *King Of America*. Only two of the twelve – by now readers will be familiar with my antipathy to *Goodbye Cruel World* and *Blood And Chocolate* – definitely fail to make the grade. Which leaves the other five fighting it out somewhere between extremely good and not bad (with *This Year's Model* at one end and *Out Of Our Idiot* at the other, I should think). Incidentally, in my view the reason for the relative failure (though it's the sort of failure almost anyone else would sell their soul to have) of these five is lack of consistency. If side two of *This Year's Model* were as good as side one then it would be up there along with *Trust*.

158

While I'm playing these games it's interesting to take a look at a similar though more ambitious game played by the staff of the *New Musical Express* in 1985 (before *King Of America*, note). They pooled their collective knowledge, opinions and prejudices to produce a list of the top 100 rock (interpreted in its broadest sense) albums in rank order. Costello fared extremely well. Five of his albums appear on the list – *Imperial Bedroom* at number thirty-one, *This Year's Model* at forty, *Get Happy!!* at sixty-eight, *Armed Forces* at ninety and *My Aim Is True* at ninety-four. As you'll notice this differs significantly from my estimation of his albums' relative merits (where the hell is *Trust?*) but makes the point that they're widely held in high esteem. Furthermore, and surprisingly, when all the nominations were totted up and a ranking list of artists (rather than albums) was compiled, Costello romped home in fourth position (after Bob Dylan, the Beatles and Marvin Gaye). So he just missed out on a medal, but still performed more than respectably when you consider the other runners' impeccable pedigrees.

His status is unarguable, even if the *NME* was perhaps being generous in placing him fourth. The really important question is, what is it that makes his songs so good? The bulk of this book is devoted to trying to explain why the best of his songs work so well, but that doesn't explain their general appeal. This is far too big an issue to hope to deal with adequately here; all I can hope to do is to provide some signposts.

In virtually all vocal music, it's the general sound that is heard first, the words usually coming second. If we don't like the music then we're unlikely to go on to listen to the words and so won't get a chance to find out whether they appeal or not. This is especially true of all forms of pop music, a genre in which on the whole words are used only because singers look silly going 'la la la' all the time. Listen to the words of the records that are in the charts as you read this and you're likely to find that ninety per cent of them are mere assemblages of clichés. So for Costello to have had any success he had to compete in this market. The secret of his success in this respect is, I think, his versatility.

His talents as a musician and as a composer of music, though by no means negligible, are not sufficiently outstanding to justify his status as one of the few great rock songwriters. He's not in the same league as Lennon and McCartney when it comes to melodic invention, for example. But he makes up for this by absorbing a wide variety of musical styles and moulding them to his own ends. It's almost true to say that every one of his albums has a different dominant style – countryish pub-rock on *My Aim Is True*, classy pop on *Armed Forces*, soul on *Get Happy!!*, country on *Almost Blue*, complex techno-pop on *Imperial Bedroom*, and so on. What's more, all these styles are adopted and adapted completely convincingly. Partly thanks to the skill of the Attractions, it almost never sounds as if we're listening to a cynical pastiche made just to cash in on the latest trend or to disguise a failure of inspiration. Costello takes these various styles and makes them his own.

The effect of this is to make the most of his already far from inconsiderable abilities as a composer of music. While it's true that for the most part the musical ideas are thinly spread, this hardly matters because we are being entertained by the varying presentation of these musical ideas. This, then, is the first reason for his general appeal: we listen to his records, at least to begin with, because musically he doesn't allow himself to get stuck in a rut so there's always something new to hear.

It has to be admitted, however, that this very versatility can backfire. Sometimes, once people have gained a taste for one phase of an artist's work, they want him to carry on producing pieces in the same vein and feel betrayed when his work evolves into something new. This is why he failed to maintain the commercial momentum he'd built up in 1978 and 79, which culminated in the enormous success of *Armed Forces* and 'Oliver's Army'. His next album was far superior, but because it was in such a radically different style he lost much of his earlier following.

Most people would agree that however good his music is it's his lyrics that really set his songs apart and make them special. As I've already noted, most pop songs are lyrically insubstantial, so however appealing they are at first, once their charm and novelty have worn off there's nothing left to hold the attention. But in the case of Costello's songs tiring of humming the tune isn't an end but a new beginning.

I must admit straight away that most of Costello's lyrics have some flaw or other in them. I'm reminded of a reviewer (I believe it was Clive James) who said of Bob Dylan's lyrics when they were first published in book form that (and I paraphrase) their tragedy was that none of the stanzas were as good as their best line, and none of the songs as good as their best stanza. Of course, this is going to be true of every song ever written unless all their lines are uniformly good (or bad, for that matter). By extension it will apply to all works of art in every medium, from *Hamlet* (which has some moderately dull passages) to an embroidered handkerchief (not every stitch of which will be precisely as good as the others). But, this said, James made a valid point. Dylan's songs, at least when read, do have a marked inconsistency. Some lines are breathtakingly good, but others are awkward and clumsy, together with all shades of grey in between. The same applies to Costello. Most of his songs contain at least one line that just doesn't seem to fit with the rest. Sometimes it sounds as if he'd thought of a line, liked it for some reason and was determined to use it whether it was really relevant or not.

Many, but by no means all, of these lapses are caused by puns and other word-play. When the puns work (as they usually do) they succeed in cramming significance into a short phrase, and so increase the song's conciseness. They're sometimes funny, too, and a sense of humour is a necessary characteristic of any great artist. But sometimes they're gratuitous and ostentatious, and hamper communication rather than enchance it. As Dr Johnson said of Shakespeare, 'A quibble [i.e. a pun] is the golden apple for which he will always turn aside from his career or stoop from his elevation . . . A quibble was to him the fatal Cleopatra for which he lost the world, and was content to lose it.' The quest for puns sometimes sidetracks Costello from the songs' main issues.

But I'm carping. I wouldn't have bothered to write this book if I thought this minor blemish seriously devalued his lyrics. Most of them are good enough to be able to withstand the odd duff line. They have a power, vision, depth and originality that can, possibly, be surpassed only by Dylan's. In a way, though, their appeal is puzzling, because the great majority of them are so depressing. *King Of America* is the only album on which happiness predominates, and even there it's a pretty close run thing. Surely there's enough misery in the world without adding to it by listening to torrents of negative emotions, however well expressed? Why on earth do we inflict this suffering on ourselves?

I think there are two linked answers to this question. Firstly, everyone feels at some time or another at least some of these negative emotions, such as rage, jealousy, hopeless love, bitterness against people who have abused their power over us. Most people probably don't feel them as intensely as the narrators of Costello's songs, and very likely don't express them with anything like the same degree of articulacy. In fact a lot of the time we don't express them at all, but bottle them up. So the songs express in an extreme form what we'd sometimes like to say if we could find the words, or what we would say if we didn't care about hurting and offending the people we'd say them to. We empathise with the narrators, who then become our spokesmen and safety-valves.

This leads us to the second answer. By listening to these deeply unhappy records we imaginatively share the narrators' feelings, and through this vicarious experience we learn. Although of course it is entirely natural to try to avoid suffering, profound unhappiness can actually be very constructive. Knowing this is no comfort when we are miserable, but nevertheless it is, I think, true. Unhappiness forces us to see things in their true perspective, and to sort out our real priorities. So the effect of listening to Costello's songs is to help us some way towards these realisations without our having to fully endure the hardships. In the final analysis, the songs are *not* depressing. After all, we see the narrators survive, and they help us survive too. Costello's persona is often on the brink but never quite topples over; we cling on with him. However much battering he takes he always pops up fighting in the next song or album; we're inspired to do the same in our own lives.

The best word to describe the effect of Costello's records on the listener is cathartic. Listening to his songs isn't completely dissimilar to watching a great tragedy, such as *King Lear*. Although at times the experiences of listening and watching verge on the unendurable, we *do* keep listening and watching. By the end we feel that we have been somehow purged of the poison in our systems, and while this process can't be properly explained it's true that we feel cleansed. This is, I think, the central fact behind the success of Costello's songs; few other rock musicians can give us such a sense of having lived and learnt.

Having made such grand claims for his music I should point out that Costello himself has never even hinted that he has any such intentions in writing his songs. On the contrary, he's always been careful to make it clear that he's not trying to be a sage or a prophet. He once said in an interview, 'I never, ever said I'm a spokesman for a generation. I never said that – thank God! I never said I'm speaking for anyone else but myself.' This is undeniably true, but nevertheless the fact remains that his deeply personal songs have touched a nerve in an age of anxiety. Almost all his songs sound as if they spring from real feelings (which is not the same thing as saying they are directly autobiographical). In the same interview he said of his songs, 'They're all personal, really. They're all from a personal point of view.' He is the Rembrandt of rock, returning over and over again to the subject of himself. This is not to accuse him of egotism, for he paints himself with merciless realism, dwelling on every wrinkle and blemish. Consequently his songs form a sequence of portraits of a man by no means always likable or admirable, but always real. They're not synthetic confections, but genuine emotional creations, and we respond to their reality.

The same note of caution about not treating him like a guru applies to his political songs. In another interview he said, 'I've never really made any claim to be changing anything,' and it's an interesting question whether anyone has had their political views altered by listening to his records. I suspect that while many of his admirers are attracted to his songs partly because they accord with leftish views, most other people, even those who listen to his records with enjoyment, are hardly aware of their political leanings. Most of his political statements are subtle and oblique: maybe the only two exceptions to this rule are 'Pills And Soap' and 'Peace In Our Time'. The others have to be listened to carefully in order to realise what he's singing about. He's not a didactic artist, ramming a message or moral down our throats. But this obliquity is a strength, not a weakness. We don't like being lectured at, and certainly don't expect records, the first function of which is to entertain, to do this. He simply expresses his own views, which we are free to take or leave, and by expressing them subtly doesn't put too many backs up. Maybe in the long run the songs even enlighten and convince some people.

What can we expect from Costello in the future? There's already been a very long pause since the release of his last album, although as I showed in the previous chapter he has by no means stopped working altogether since *Blood And Chocolate*. He could be, and I very much hope this is the case, just taking a well deserved rest. He was a musical workaholic for a decade, and no one will begrudge him a break from what must become the annual grind of having to make a new album. The few reports that come in about him confirm that he is still writing songs, including one on the subject of capital punishment, apparently. He still supports leftish causes – he played a benefit concert for striking seamen in the summer of 1988. What I should like to see him do, of course, is to return to making albums, though perhaps not as frequently as before. If this happens, as seems likely, it would be good to see him take up from where *King Of America* left off and explore subjects and styles he hasn't yet touched. In particular, I'd prefer him to expand the thematic range of his songs (the one about capital punishment sounds promising). One criticism that can be levelled against his work, especially when you compare him with someone like Dylan who admittedly has been making records for a lot longer, is that he tends to cover similar ground rather often. Tortured relationships, exposés of the media and big business and so on are excellent subjects and can provide material for very many more songs, but it would be great to see him branch out and surprise everyone with a totally different record.

Over the years he's demonstrated his staying power, but almost inevitably the time will come when his creative powers dry up. This has been the destiny of virtually all other rock musicians, usually sooner rather than later. It is possible, though unlikely, that he's more or less reached that stage now. It could even be that his personal life has reached an equilibrium and so he no longer has the creative urge. After all, 'Everyday I Write The Book' seems to imply that his compositions spring from feelings of 'longing', and if he no longer has these feelings perhaps he lacks inspiration. The process of artistic creation is a mysterious one. But whatever the case, I wish him well. Even if his career as a songwright (a maker of songs as a wheelwright is a maker of wheels) is over, which I doubt, his achievement is unassailable. His albums guarantee him a place on the top table at rock's banquet. As long as rock music is listened to it seems very likely that his records will continue to be played and appreciated. There is no truly objective test of art's worth, but the closest thing there is to one is whether a work lasts or not. While it's impossible to know if Costello's songs will stand the test of time, if any rock songs deserve to last, his do. Their themes are universal and so will speak to the future as they speak to us in the present. His appeal is not limited by passing fads and fashions, but is based on firmer, permanent foundations. He is a man out of time.

Appendix

The Best of Elvis Costello

The purpose of this appendix is to annoy the reader. The thirty-six songs are, in my opinion, the best of Elvis Costello. In other words, they're my favourites. No two people will ever be in complete agreement on such a subjective issue. I've made several drafts of this list, each time with a slightly different result according to my mood. Nevertheless I think it's a useful exercise and maybe a good starting point for discussions.

Why thirty-six songs? No very special reason, but three dozen seems a nice round figure, also it's big enough to include a wide cross-section of Costello's work, and small enough to exclude the good-but-not-brilliant. I believe that all the songs listed here, even if some of them are flawed in one way or another, are state-of-the-art rock songs. I haven't considered cover versions for inclusion.

If you like you can imagine the songs below as the contents of a double album with nine songs per side; good value, I think. I've put an asterisk next to the eighteen songs that I'd choose if I were forced to cut my selection down to the size of a single album – the *very* best of Elvis Costello.

1. 'No Dancing'
2. 'Alison'*
3. '(The Angels Want to Wear My) Red Shoes'
4. 'Watching the Detectives'*
5. 'This Year's Girl'
6. 'The Beat'
7. 'Pump It Up'*
8. 'Radio Radio'
9. 'Accidents Will Happen'*
10. 'Oliver's Army'*
11. 'Black And White World'*
12. 'Five Gears In Reverse'
13. 'Opportunity'*
14. 'The Imposter'
15. 'King Horse'*

16. 'Man Called Uncle'
17. 'Hoover Factory'
18. 'Just A Memory'*
19. 'Clubland'*
20. 'You'll Never Be A Man'
21. 'New Lace Sleeves'
22. 'Shot With His Own Gun'
23. 'Big Sister's Clothes'*
24. 'The Long Honeymoon'
25. 'Man Out Of Time'*
26. 'Almost Blue'*
27. 'Kid About It'*
28. 'You Little Fool'*
29. 'Imperial Bedroom'
30. 'Everyday I Write The Book'
31. 'Shipbuilding'*
32. 'The Invisible Man'
33. 'Brilliant Mistake'
34. 'Glitter Gulch'
35. 'American Without Tears'*
36. 'Poisoned Rose'*

Bibliography

Elvis Costello – A Completely False Biography Based on Rumour, Innuendo and Lies by Krista Reese, Proteus, 1981
Contains some good pictures, otherwise worthless.

Elvis Costello – The Illustrated Disco/Biography by Geoff Parkyn, Omnibus, 1984
Contains a complete discography up to and including *Goodbye Cruel World*, also some publicity photos, and a short introduction mainly concerning the critical reception of Costello's songs. Ignore the 'Biography' part of the title – this seems to be simply an attempt on the part of Costello's management to preempt other possible biographers.

Elvis Costello – An Illustrated Biography by Mick St Michael, Omnibus, 1986
Readable and useful, but makes no attempt to be definitive.

Elvis Costello – A Singing Dictionary, Plangent Visions, 1980
Contains all the music and lyrics for the original songs from *My Aim Is True, This Year's Model, Armed Forces, Get Happy!!* and *Ten Bloody Marys And Ten How's Your Fathers*, plus one unrecorded song.

Elvis Costello – Everyday I Write The Song (Grumbling Appendix To the Singing Dictionary), Plangent Visions, 1983
Contains all the music and lyrics from *Trust, Imperial Bedroom* and *Punch The Clock*. This and the previous volume are the only printed sources of the lyrics before *Imperial Bedroom*, and are thus invaluable to anyone seriously interested in Costello's songs.

Discography

This list contains all Costello's major UK releases, but makes no attempt to include reissues, promotional copies, etc. Geoff Parkyn has compiled a complete discography (see bibliography).

	Date	Record Label
Singles		
'Less Than Zero'/'Radio Sweetheart'	77	Stiff
'Alison'/'Welcome to the Working Week'	77	Stiff
'Red Shoes'/'Mystery Dance'	77	Stiff
'Watching the Detectives'/'Blame It On Cain' (live)/'Mystery Dance' (live)	77	Stiff
'(I Don't Want To Go To) Chelsea'/'You Belong To Me'	78	Radar
'Stranger in the House'/'Neat Neat Neat' (live) [free with early copies of *This Year's Model*]	78	Radar
'Pump It Up'/'Big Tears'	78	Radar
'Radio Radio'/'Tiny Steps'	78	Radar
'Oliver's Army'/'My Funny Valentine'	79	Radar
'Watching the Detectives' (live)/'Alison' (live)/'Accidents Will Happen' (live) [the 'Live At The Hollywood High' EP, free with early copies of *Armed Forces*]	79	Radar
'Accidents Will Happen'/'Talking In The Dark'/'Wednesday Week'	79	Radar
'I Can't Stand Up For Falling Down'/'Girls Talk'	80	F-Beat

169

'High Fidelity'/'Getting Mighty Crowded'/'Clowntime Is Over' No. 2 (12-inch only)	80	F-Beat
'New Amsterdam'/'Dr Luther's Assistant'/'Ghost Train'/'Just A Memory' (EP only)	80	F-Beat
'Clubland'/'Clean Money'/'Hoover Factory'	80	F-Beat
'From A Whisper To A Scream'/'Luxembourg'	81	F-Beat
'Good Year For the Roses'/'Your Angel Steps Out of Heaven'	81	F-Beat
'Sweet Dreams'/'Psycho' (live)	81	F-Beat
'I'm Your Toy' (live)/B-side includes 'Cry Cry Cry'/'Wondering' (7-inch only), 'My Shoes Keep Walking Back To You'/'Blues Keep Calling'/'Honky Tonk Girl' (12-inch only)	82	F-Beat
'You Little Fool'/'Big Sister'/'Stamping Ground'	82	F-Beat
'Man Out Of Time'/'Town Cryer' No. 2/'Imperial Bedroom' (12-inch only)	82	F-Beat
'From Head to Toe'/'The World of Broken Hearts'	82	F-Beat
'Party Party'/'Imperial Bedroom'	82	A&M
'Pills And Soap'	83	Imp
'Everyday I Write The Book'/'Heathen Town'/+ 'Night Time' (12-inch only)	83	F-Beat
'Let Them All Talk'/'The Flirting Kind' (12-inch features extended A-side)	83	F-Beat
'Peace In Our Time'/'Withered and Died'	84	Imp
'I Wanna Be Loved'/'Turning the Town Red'	84	F-Beat
'The Only Flame in Town'/'The Comedians' (12-inch features a 'version discotheque' of A-side, 'Pump It Up'/'Baby It's You' replacing 'The Comedians')	84	F-Beat
'The People's Limousine'/'They'll Never Take Her Love From Me' (as The Coward Brothers, with T-Bone Burnett)	85	Imp
'Don't Let Me Be Misunderstood'/'Baby's Got a Brand New Hairdo'	86	F-Beat
'Tokyo Storm Warning'/+ 'Black Sails In The Sunset' (12-inch only)	86	Imp
'I Want You'/'I Hope You're Happy Now'	86	Imp

'Blue Chair'/'American Without Tears' No. 2   87   Demon
(Twilight Version)/+ 'Shoes Without
Heels'/'American Without Tears' (12-inch
only)

Albums

My Aim Is True	77	Stiff
This Year's Model	78	Radar
Armed Forces	79	Radar
Get Happy!!	80	F-Beat
Ten Bloody Marys and Ten How's Your	80	F-Beat
Fathers (originally cassette only)		
Trust	81	F-Beat
Almost Blue	81	F-Beat
Imperial Bedroom	82	F-Beat
Punch The Clock	83	F-Beat
Goodbye Cruel World	84	F-Beat
The Best of Elvis Costello – The Man	85	Telstar
King Of America	86	F-Beat
Blood And Chocolate	86	Demon
Out Of Our Idiot	87	Demon

Costello's back catalogue has now been reissued by Demon records. Also of interest are:

The Courier (most of side two composed but not performed by Costello; all instrumental)	88	Virgin
Nothing But the Truth (Rubén Blades; two songs co-written by Costello)	88	Elektra

A video tape of the promotional videos made for Costello's songs is available.